AMERICA'S MODERN POETIC VOICES IN A HALF CENTURY OF VERSE

Emphatically eclectic, this broad, rich collection offers readers a comprehensive survey of twentieth-century American poetry—and great poems to fit any taste, mood, time of day, or season of life.

If your spirits need a lift, turn to X. J. Kennedy's "In a Prominent Bar in Secaucus One Day" and sing its bawdy verses out loud to the tune of "Sweet Betsy from Pike." Looking for the right words to capture the melancholy of an autumn afternoon? Read Robert Nathan's "Now Blue October" or Margaret Gibson's "October Elegy." Feeling wry and whimsical? John Updike's "Telephone Poles" remarks on the world we have made; dark and contemplative? Sylvia Plath's "Last Words" reveals her continuing love affair with death; mischievous and iconoclastic? George Starbuck's "The Spell Against Spelling" assails the Miss Grundys everywhere.

Fifty Years of American Poetry is an outstanding collection of the best work of America's most esteemed modern poets.

FIFTY YEARS OF AMERICAN POETRY

FROM THE ACADEMY OF AMERICAN POETS

Fifty Years of American Poetry

ANNIVERSARY VOLUME FOR THE ACADEMY OF AMERICAN POETS

INTRODUCTION BY
ROBERT PENN WARREN

A LAUREL BOOK

Published by
Dell Publishing
a division of
Bantam Doubleday Dell Publishing Group, Inc.
1540 Broadway
New York, New York 10036

Published by arrangement with The Philip Lief Group, Inc.
6 West 20th Street
New York, New York 10011

ISBN: 0-440-21877-2

Reprinted by arrangement with Harry N. Abrams, Inc.

Printed in the United States of America

Published simultaneously in Canada

September 1995

10 9 8 7 6 5 4 3 2

OPM

CONTENTS

INTRODUCTION

This is the semi-centennial of The Academy of American Poets, and this anthology, created at the suggestion of Harry N. Abrams, Inc., the distinguished publishing house, and the Book-of-the-Month Club, is one of the various celebrations of that event. In it are represented, with one poem each, the Chancellors, Fellows, and Award Winners since 1934—a hundred and twenty-six poets in all—a sort of cross-section of American poetry in the last half-century. A glance at the table of contents will show that no one school, bailiwick, method, or category of poetry has dominated the interest of the Academy. The Academy has been interested in poetry, not in cults or schools, in helping, as best it could, though no doubt with some human failing, serious poets of whatsoever persuasion.

What does the Academy do? According to its certificate of incorporation, its purpose is "To encourage, stimulate, and foster the production of American poetry. . . ." The responsibility for its activities lies with the Board of Directors (with Mrs. Hugh Bullock as president and many board members of distinguished reputation) and the Board of twelve Chancellors, which has included, over the years, such figures as Louise Bogan, W.H. Auden, Witter Bynner, Randall Jarrell, Robert Lowell, Robinson Jeffers, Marianne Moore, James Merrill, Robert Fitzgerald, F.O. Matthiessen, and Archibald MacLeish—certainly not members of the same poetic church. The primary duty of the Chancellors is to determine the winners of the various Fellowship Awards and, upon request, to advise the Board of Directors. As for the Fellowships, from 1937 to 1969, the value of each was $5,000, and since then $10,000. The first Fellowship was awarded in 1947 to Edgar Lee Masters, a prefatory award having been made in 1937 to Edwin Markham. To date there are forty-seven Fellows.

Very significantly, the Academy has tried to reach beyond the professional level to the young, from whom the new poets must spring, or the new readers of poetry. For instance, the program of Poetry-in-the-Schools, fostered by the Academy, is now national. Furthermore, the Academy has assumed that its mission is not "Eastern provincial," as the awards and the books vouched for by the Academy and its various other activities clearly show. Behind all of these lies the assumption that poetry is not for poets only, but for readers, and that the cultivation of readers—the explanation of what poetry really is, what and how it "means," what it is about, how it may affect the reader—is essential for the health of poetry.

American education has become debased in this department since the old-fashioned days when, in almost all grades, there were usually required recitations of memorized poems, and often a discussion of them. We may compare the present perfunctory attention to poetry to the French system by which poems, even in early grades, simple for the very young, but by a master, must be memorized each week, recited, and then analyzed in a written theme based on specific questions. To have great poets there must be great audiences, Whitman said, to the more or less unheeding ears of American educators. Ambitiously, hopefully, the Academy has undertaken to remedy this plight.

Let us look back a half century to the moment in which the Academy was founded. At that time the modern poetic revolution was already here. Robinson, the forerunner, had only a year or so to live. Frost was at the height of his fame, as was Eliot. Hart Crane was already dead. Ransom had written most of his poems. William Carlos Williams published his first *Collected Poems*, with an introduction by Wallace Stevens, almost simultaneously with the founding of the Academy. A new generation, offspring of that revolution, was about to appear.

The fact of such a background in no way diminishes the importance of the founding of the Academy, even though it may have given preparation for it. To those already sunk in poetry, it had been an exhilarating period, but many literates, or semi-such readers, and many established professors had not heard the news (except for Robinson and Frost, and more remotely the rumor of Eliot), or took it as bad news. There were not many F.O. Matthiessens and Cleanth Brookses around in those days. Furthermore, most graduate students, even in important universities, were above such trivialities, a fact I can vouch for from my own experience. In other words, most of the poetic ferment had been in the scum afloat at the top of the pot and not in the heart of the brew. This is not, however, to say that many writers or readers who felt the necessity of the achievements of modernism were not solidly, or adequately, grounded in the old literature and devoted to it. They simply felt, instinctively, that literature must be a constantly expanding growth in a world of inevitable change. The Academy recognized the inevitability of change, and that literature is an expanding growth, as the limited tenure of Chancellors most obviously testifies. The poetry of today is not that of the 1920s and 1930s, and certain contemporary poets of real achievement find little or no direct inspiration from that earlier revolution.

If we look for the genesis of the Academy, we see a young woman, Marie Graves, of French birth but American parentage, raised in France (except for the years of World War I), steeped in music from all the festivals of Europe, from study, and from the musicians, along with artists and writers, frequenting the house of her family, and those of their friends. And there was, too, the Sorbonne.

When, in 1933, she married an American, Mr. Hugh Bullock, and came to New York, she was in for a surprise. "I found no poets (or other artists) at social events I attended in New York City, as I had done constantly on the Continent; and when poets I had looked forward to hearing in class [she had registered at Columbia] were not given time off from such jobs as soda-fountain jerk, or salesman in a clothing store, to come and read, my sense of artistic appreciation, nurtured in Europe, was immensely outraged."

She knew, of course, that things much more important than social life were involved; that situation was merely a symptom. Life itself—bread—was involved. Poverty was a common lot for poets unless they had the stamina to carry a job, menial or not, or a profession, with poetry an occupation of stolen time. Yes, there had been hungry and shabby poets even in France—the Nervals and Verlaines, the poets *maudits*. (Though Verlaine, in old age, did receive some private help.) And the same was true of England, from Chatterton to Francis Thompson, for example. The Continent was a little short of Utopia. But on that Continent there was a much more widespread, even official, recognition of poetry, and the other arts, as a basic national asset. In the early 1930s, a friend of mine, a poet of high reputation, was living with his family in a small French village, where he was often seen publicly carrying garbage from the kitchen. A delegation of the ladies of the village called on my friend's wife, and finally worked up the courage to tell her that it was not seemly for a poet to be seen in that role; it gave the village a bad name. Comedy, yes. But something else, too.

Even though poetry was regarded in various European countries as a national asset, prime ministers and bureaucrats did not necessarily retain much more than the fading recollection of it from the lycée or university; however, they knew an asset when they saw it. And a number of high officials have been writers of stature, most recently and famously St. John Perse as a poet, and Winston Churchill as a historian and prose stylist.

The long tradition of patronage, as Mrs. Bullock well knew, runs from the Greeks to modern Europe, accounting, quite literally, for many world masterpieces. Though the private patron survived, the governments themselves were assuming more and more responsibility. In England, from the late Middle Ages, private bounty was not uncommon and eventually the Crown provided substantial subsidy, and in the following centuries, along with much important private munificence, there was a drift toward a consistent governmental patronage, ending in the annual Civil List—where once a name is inscribed, an annuity follows for life.

It is true that in America, in the nineteenth century, the government occasionally appointed a literary man to a post at home, most famously the Custom House, or abroad as a consul, Hawthorne having served, not always happily or productively, in both capacities. But we remember that the great Melville, fallen on evil days, served in the Custom House in New York—though not as a political appointee—grubbing away for many years at $4.00 a day, working at his poetry at night.

It was not until Theodore Roosevelt that an American poet received government patronage with any degree of understanding. When Robinson was in middle life, the author of only two books, a son of Roosevelt called the president's attention to one of them, *Children of the Night,* which the youth admired. The father, that strange combination of a sprawling diversity of qualities, recognized the talent in the poems and arranged an interview with the poet in which he said, "I regret that no Civil List exists in this country as in England and elsewhere. In its absence, I am forced to offer you a post in the Custom House. If you accept it, I urge you to put poetry first and the United States Treasury second." Apparently Robinson followed that advice, and a score of volumes followed—and great fame.

Theodore Roosevelt has had no successor of the same kidney.

Our government has, however, lately shown a new awareness of the arts, and has a number of very definite achievements to its credit. We should, of course, be grateful for this fact, and should hope for permanence and development. But should we assume that a political solution, however high-minded, is adequate? Certainly such a program would be the most vulnerable when budget-cutters get to work. That, however, is not my real point. Private aid to the arts seems to be more in the American individualistic tradition. Even a great foundation represents an individual's sense of values. And the individual who writes a $10.00 check for The Academy of American Poets has, however slightly, a new relation to the art of poetry; it is, in a sense, "his." This is not to say that poetry or the reading of it should be the primary concern of mankind: but it is an activity, for writer or reader, valuable and unique, and a fundamental measure of the quality of any civilization.

I may seem to have wandered far from the founding of the Academy, but much of what I have said presumably lies in the background of that event, and in the Founder's determination, in her first distress about the American scene, to try "to do something about it." First, for discussion and advice, she turned to the poets she had, in fact, met, among whom were Robinson, Ridgely Torrence (poetry editor of the *New Republic*), Joseph Auslander (a teacher of hers at Columbia). Then, on the practical side, there was her husband, with his knowledge of the world of finance and law (and whose commitment was to grow to the point where he served as Secretary of the Academy). Those early days of struggle and hope come now to the Founder's mind: "We used many odd means to try to secure interest and funds. . . . It was hard work. I well remember the first early contributions, and how exciting it was to receive the first $50.00 or $100.00 check. And how much it meant when a bricklayer sent a $1.00 bill, because he 'loved poetry.' " It is easy to understand the symbolic weight of that $1.00, a meaning deeper, and more justifying, than that of munificent impersonal gifts from great corporations or foundations or governmental agencies.

The Academy has long since become a significant American institution. The originally vague, but dauntless, impulse "to do something about it" took form, bit by bit, with the aid of many other dauntless hearts and able workers. And here should be mentioned Elizabeth Kray, who, for many years, ingeniously and devotedly committed herself and her great skills to the office of Executive Director.

It is hard to think back to the time, which some of us can still remember, when a public poetry reading was a rarity and, when one did occur, was often the subject of a jest. But now they are numberless, good and bad, in all sorts of places, and usually to well populated or packed houses. And not uncommonly universities, great and famous or small, welcome poets to their faculties. But these items are merely symptoms of a change in American society—society in the broadest sense—to which the Academy has so vitally con-

PREFACE

On November 7, 1934, The Academy of American Poets was incorporated in Albany, New York, as a "Membership Corporation." Thus began an exciting fifty years of activity to secure assistance for programs for poetry.

It wasn't easy. Poets had not taken their place in the American way of life. The average American did not reel off poems the way Italians knew Dante from memory and French people recited Racine and Corneille or the more lyric Alfred de Musset, or the British quoted Shakespeare and Byron.

Walt Whitman had made a deep impression but Emerson's easiest lines repeated often were usually prose, and except for parroting Poe's "Raven," nobody thought much about American poetry. Life was too busy.

Nevertheless in these fifty years The Academy of American Poets has awarded forty-seven Fellowships totaling over $300,000; awarded thirty Lamont Poetry Selection prizes, ten Walt Whitman Awards, and five Landon Translation Award books each with $1,000 prizes.

The College Poetry Prizes, established in 1954 with ten awards, now function in 131 universities and colleges and annually draw 4,000 competitors.

The Academy also initiated the first Poetry-in-the-Schools program and a number of other activities all over the United States. Poetry readings, historical presentations, walks, and especially Affiliated Societies are numbered amongst these.

In this Fiftieth Anniversary year, celebrated nationally by libraries and individuals, the Academy seeks to tell of its appreciation to the many people and organizations who have helped us on our way.

We particularly thank our Chancellors and Fellows who

The Poems

E. A. ROBINSON

For a Dead Lady 1

No more with overflowing light
Shall fill the eyes that now are faded,
Nor shall another's fringe with night
Their woman-hidden world as they did.

No more shall quiver down the days
The flowing wonder of her ways,
Whereof no language may requite
The shifting and the many-shaded.

The grace, divine, definitive,
Clings only as a faint forestalling;
The laugh that love could not forgive
Is hushed, and answers to no calling;
The forehead and the little ears
Have gone where Saturn keeps the years;
The breast where roses could not live
Has done with rising and with falling.

The beauty, shattered by the laws
That have creation in their keeping,
No longer trembles at applause,
Or over children that are sleeping;
And we who delve in beauty's lore
Know all that we have known before
Of what inexorable cause
Makes Time so vicious in his reaping.

EDGAR LEE MASTERS

The Hill 2

Where are Elmer, Herman, Bert, Tom and Charley,
The weak of will, the strong of arm, the clown, the
    boozer, the fighter?
All, all, are sleeping on the hill.

One passed in a fever,
One was burned in a mine,
One was killed in a brawl,
One died in a jail,
One fell from a bridge toiling for children and wife—
All, all are sleeping, sleeping, sleeping on the hill.

Where are Ella, Kate, Mag, Lizzie and Edith,
The tender heart, the simple soul, the loud, the proud,
    the happy one?—
All, all, are sleeping on the hill.

One died in shameful child-birth
One of a thwarted love,
One at the hands of a brute in a brothel,
One of a broken pride, in the search for her heart's
    desire,
One after life in far-away London and Paris
Was brought to her little space by Ella and Kate and
    Mag—
All, all are sleeping, sleeping, sleeping on the hill.

Where are Uncle Isaac and Aunt Emily,
And old Towny Kincaid and Sevigne Houghton,
And Major Walker who had talked
With venerable men of the revolution—
All, all, are sleeping on the hill.

They brought them dead sons from the war,
And daughters whom life had crushed,
And their children fatherless, crying—
All, all are sleeping, sleeping, sleeping on the hill.

Where is Old Fiddler Jones
Who played with life all his ninety years,
Braving the sleet with bared breast,
Drinking, rioting, thinking neither of wife nor kin,
Nor gold, nor love, nor heaven?
Lo! he babbles of the fish-frys of long ago,
Of the horse-races of long ago at Clary's Grove,
Of what Abe Lincoln said
One time at Springfield.

EZRA POUND

The River-Merchant's Wife: A Letter 4

While my hair was still cut straight across my forehead
Played I about the front gate, pulling flowers.
You came by on bamboo stilts, playing horse,
You walked about my seat, playing with blue plums.
And we went on living in the village of Chokan:
Two small people, without dislike or suspicion.

At fourteen I married My Lord you.
I never laughed, being bashful.
Lowering my head, I looked at the wall.
Called to, a thousand times, I never looked back.

At fifteen I stopped scowling,
I desired my dust to be mingled with yours
Forever and forever and forever.
Why should I climb the look out?

At sixteen you departed,
You went into far Ku-to-yen, by the river of swirling eddies,
And you have been gone five months.
The monkeys make sorrowful noise overhead.

You dragged your feet when you went out.
By the gate now, the moss is grown, the different mosses,
Too deep to clear them away!
The leaves fall early this autumn, in wind.
The paired butterflies are already yellow with August
Over the grass in the West garden;
They hurt me. I grow older.

If you are coming down through the narrows of the river
Kiang,
Please let me know beforehand,
And I will come out to meet you
As far as Cho-fu-Sa.

PADRAIC COLUM

An Old Woman of the Roads 6

Oh, to have a little house!
To own the hearth and stool and all!
The heaped-up sods upon the fire,
The pile of turf against the wall!

To have a clock with weights and chains
And pendulum swinging up and down,
A dresser filled with shining delph,
Speckled and white and blue and brown!

I could be busy all the day
Clearing and sweeping hearth and floor,
And fixing on their shelf again
My white and blue and speckled store!

I could be quiet there at night
Beside the fire and by myself,
Sure of a bed and loth to leave
The ticking clock and the shining delph!

Och! but I'm weary of mist and dark,
And roads where there's never a house nor bush,
And tired I am of bog and road,
And the crying wind and the lonesome hush!

And I am praying to God on high,
And I am praying him night and day,
For a little house, a house of my own—
Out of the wind's and the rain's way.

WITTER BYNNER

Driftwood 7

Come, warm your hands
From the cold wind of time.
I have built here under the moon,
A many-coloured fire
With fragments of wood
That have been part of a tree
And part of a ship.

Were leaves more real,
Or driven nails,
Or fingers of builders,
Than these burning violets?
Come, warm your hands
From the cold wind of time.
There's a fire under the moon.

CONRAD AIKEN

Preludes for Memnon, II 8

Two coffees in the Español, the last
Bright drops of golden Barsac in a goblet,
Fig paste and candied nuts . . . Hardy is dead,
And James and Conrad dead, and Shakspere dead,
And old Moore ripens for an obscene grave,
And Yeats for an arid one; and I, and you—
What winding sheet for us, what boards and bricks,
What mummeries, candles, prayers, and pious frauds?
You shall be lapped in Syrian scarlet, woman,
And wear your pearls, and your bright bracelets, too,
Your agate ring, and round your neck shall hang
Your dark blue lapis with its specks of gold.
And I, beside you—ah! but will that be?
For there are dark streams in this dark world, lady,
Gulf Streams and Arctic currents of the soul;
And I may be, before our consummation
Beds us together, cheek by jowl, in earth,
Swept to another shore, where my white bones
Will lie unhonored, or defiled by gulls.

What dignity can death bestow on us,
Who kiss beneath a streetlamp, or hold hands
Half hidden in a taxi, or replete
With coffee, figs and Barsac make our way
To a dark bedroom in a wormworn house?
The aspidistra guards the door; we enter,
Per aspidistra—then—*ad astra*—is it?—
And lock ourselves securely in our gloom
And loose ourselves from terror. . . . Here's my hand,
The white scar on my thumb, and here's my mouth
To stop your murmur; speechless let us lie,
And think of Hardy, Shakspere, Yeats and James;
Comfort our panic hearts with magic names;

Stare at the ceiling, where the taxi lamps
Make ghosts of light; and see, beyond this bed,
That other bed in which we will not move;
And, whether joined or separated, will not love.

JOSEPH AUSLANDER

Interval 10

Water pulls nervously whispering satin across cool roots, cold stones;
And a bird balances his soul on a song flash, a desperate outcry:
These are the minor chords, the monotones;
This the undefeated gesture against an armored sky.

The moment is metal; the sun crawling over it is a fly
Head down on a bronze ceiling; the hot stillness drones:
And you go sliding through green sea shafts and I
Am an old mountain warming his tired bones.

JOHN CROWE RANSOM

Judith of Bethulia

Beautiful as the flying legend of some leopard
She had not yet chosen her great captain or prince
Depositary to her flesh, and our defense;
And a wandering beauty is a blade out of its scabbard.
You know how dangerous, gentlemen of threescore?
May you know it yet ten more.

Nor by process of veiling she grew the less fabulous.
Grey or blue veils, we were desperate to study
The invincible emanations of her white body,
And the winds at her ordered raiment were ominous.
Might she walk in the market, sit in the council of
    soldiers?
Only of the extreme elders.

But a rare chance was the girl's then, when the Invader
Trumpeted from the south, and rumbled from the north,
Beleaguered the city from four quarters of the earth,
Our soldiery too craven and sick to aid her—
Where were the arms could countervail this horde?
Her beauty was the sword.

She sat with the elders, and proved on their blear visage
How bright was the weapon unrusted in her keeping,
While he lay surfeiting on their harvest heaping,
Wasting the husbandry of their rarest vintage—
And dreaming of the broad-breasted dames for
    concubine?
These floated on his wine.

He was lapped with bay-leaves, and grass and fumiter
    weed,

And from under the wine-film encountered his mortal
vision,
For even within his tent she accomplished his derision;
She loosed one veil and another, standing unafraid;
And he perished. Nor brushed her with even so much as
a daisy?
She found his destruction easy.

The heathen are all perished. The victory was furnished,
We smote them hiding in our vineyards, barns, annexes,
And now their white bones clutter the holes of foxes,
And the chieftain's head, with grinning sockets, and
varnished—
Is it hung on the sky with a hideous epitaphy?
No, the woman keeps the trophy.

May God send unto our virtuous lady her prince.
It is stated she went reluctant to that orgy,
Yet a madness fevers our young men, and not the clergy
Nor the elders have turned them unto modesty since.
Inflamed by the thought of her naked beauty with desire?
Yes, and chilled with fear and despair.

WILLIAM ROSE BENÉT

Jesse James 13
(A Design in Red and Yellow for a Nickel Library)

JESSE JAMES was a two-gun man,
    (Roll on, Missouri!)
Strong-arm chief of an outlaw clan.
    (From Kansas to Illinois!)
He twirled an old Colt forty-five;
    (Roll on, Missouri!)
They never took Jesse James alive.
    (Roll, Missouri, roll!)

Jesse James was King of the Wes';
    (Cataracks in the Missouri!)
He'd a di'mon' heart in his lef' breas';
    (Brown Missouri rolls!)
He'd a fire in his heart no hurt could stifle;
    (Thunder, Missouri!)
Lion eyes an' a Winchester rifle.
    (Missouri, roll down!)

Jesse James rode a pinto hawse;
Come at night to a water-cawse;
Tetched with the rowel that pinto's flank;
She sprung the torrent from bank to bank.

Jesse rode through a sleepin' town;
Looked the moonlit street both up an' down;
Crack-crack-crack, the street ran flames
An' a great voice cried, "I'm Jesse James!"

Hawse an' afoot they're after Jess!
    (Roll on, Missouri!)
Spurrin' an' spurrin'—but he's gone Wes'.
    (Brown Missouri rolls!)

He was ten foot tall when he stood in his boots;
(Lightnin' light the Missouri!)
More'n a match fer sich galoots.
(Roll, Missouri, roll!)

Jesse James rode outa the sage;
Roun' the rocks come the swayin' stage;
Straddlin' the road a giant stan's
An' a great voice bellers, "Throw up yer han's!"

Jesse raked in the di'mon' rings,
The big gold watches an' the yuther things;
Jesse divvied 'em then an' thar
With a cryin' child had lost her mar.

The U.S. troopers is after Jess;
(Roll on, Missouri!)
Their hawses sweat foam, but he's gone Wes';
(Hear Missouri roar!)
He was broad as a b'ar, he'd a ches' like a drum,
(Wind an' rain through Missouri!)
An' his red hair flamed like Kingdom Come.
(Missouri down to the sea!)

Jesse James all alone in the rain
Stopped an' stuck up the Eas'-boun' train;
Swayed through the coaches with horns an' a tail,
Lit out with the bullion an' the registered mail.

Jess made 'em all turn green with fright
Quakin' in the aisles in the pitch-black night;
An' he give all the bullion to a pore ole tramp
Campin' nigh the cuttin' in the dirt an' damp.

The whole U. S. is after Jess;
(Roll on, Missouri!)
The son-of-a-gun, if he ain't gone Wes';
(Missouri to the sea!)
He could chaw cold iron an' spit blue flame;
(Cataracks down the Missouri!)
He rode on a catamount he'd larned to tame.
(Hear that Missouri roll!)

Jesse James rode into a bank;
Give his pinto a tetch on the flank;
Jumped the teller's window with an awful crash;
Heaved up the safe an' twirled his mustache;

He said, "So long, boys!" He yelped, "So long!
Feelin' porely today—I ain't feelin' strong!"
Rode right through the wall a-goin' crack-crack-crack—
Took the safe home to mother in a gunny-sack.

They're creepin', they're crawlin', they're stalkin' Jess;
(Roll on, Missouri!)
They's a rumor he's gone much further Wes';
(Roll, Missouri, roll!)
They's word of a cayuse hitched to the bars
(Ruddy clouds on Missouri!)
Of a golden sunset that busts into stars.
(Missouri, roll down!)

Jesse James rode hell fer leather;
He was a hawse an' a man together;
In a cave in a mountain high up in air
He lived with a rattlesnake, a wolf, an' a bear.

Jesse's heart was as sof' as a woman;
Fer guts an' stren'th he was sooper-human;
He could put six shots through a woodpecker's eye
And take in one swaller a gallon o' rye.

They sought him here an' they sought him there,
    (*Roll on, Missouri!*)
But he strides by night through the ways of the air;
    (*Brown Missouri rolls!*)
They say he was took an' they say he is dead,
    (*Thunder, Missouri!*)
But he ain't—he's a sunset overhead!
    (*Missouri down to the sea!*)

Jesse James was a Hercules.
When he went through the woods he tore up the trees.
When he went on the plains he smoked the groun'
An' the hull lan' shuddered fer miles aroun'.

Jesse James wore a red bandanner
That waved on the breeze like the Star Spangled Banner;
In seven states he cut up dadoes.
He's gone with the buffler an' the desperadoes.

Yes, Jesse James was a two-gun man
    (*Roll on, Missouri!*)
The same as when this song began;
    (*From Kansas to Illinois!*)
An' when you see a sunset bust into flames
    (*Lightnin' light the Missouri!*)
Or a thunderstorm blaze—that's Jesse James!
    (*Hear that Missouri roll!*)

ROBINSON JEFFERS

Hurt Hawks 17

I

The broken pillar of the wing jags from the clotted shoulder,
The wing trails like a banner in defeat,
No more to use the sky forever but live with famine
And pain a few days: cat nor coyote
Will shorten the week of waiting for death, there is game without talons.
He stands under the oak-bush and waits
The lame feet of salvation; at night he remembers freedom
And flies in a dream, the dawns ruin it.
He is strong and pain is worse to the strong, incapacity is worse.
The curs of the day come and torment him
At distance, no one but death the redeemer will humble that head,
The intrepid readiness, the terrible eyes.
The wild God of the world is sometimes merciful to those
That ask mercy, not often to the arrogant.
You do not know him, you communal people, or you have forgotten him;
Intemperate and savage, the hawk remembers him;
Beautiful and wild, the hawks, and men that are dying, remember him.

II

I'd sooner, except the penalties, kill a man than a hawk; but the great redtail
Had nothing left but unable misery
From the bone too shattered for mending, the wing that trailed under his talons when he moved.

We had fed him six weeks, I gave him freedom,
He wandered over the foreland hill and returned in the
    evening, asking for death,
Not like a beggar, still eyed with the old
Implacable arrogance. I gave him the lead gift in the
    twilight. What fell was relaxed,
Owl-downy, soft feminine feathers; but what
Soared: the fierce rush: the night-herons by the flooded
    river cried fear at its rising
Before it was quite unsheathed from reality.

The Cameo

Forever over now, forever, forever gone
That day. Clear and diminished like a scene
Carven in cameo, the lighthouse, and the cove between
The sandy cliffs, and the boat drawn up on the beach;
And the long skirt of a lady innocent and young,
Her hand resting on her bosom, her head hung;
And the figure of a man in earnest speech.

Clear and diminished like a scene cut in cameo
The lighthouse, and the boat on the beach, and the two
    shapes
Of the woman and the man; lost like the lost day
Are the words that passed, and the pain,—discarded, cut
    away
From the stone, as from the memory the heat of the tears
    escapes.

O troubled forms, O early love unfortunate and hard,
Time has estranged you into a jewel cold and pure;
From the action of the waves and from the action of
    sorrow forever secure,
White against a ruddy cliff you stand, chalcedony on sard.

OLIVER ST. JOHN GOGARTY

Anachronism 20

Tall and great-bearded: black and white,
The deep-eyed beggar gazed about,
For all his weight of years, upright;
He woke the morning with a shout,
One shout, one note, one rolling word;
But in my dreaming ears I heard
The sea-filled rhythm roll again,
And saw long-vanished boys and men
With eager faces ranged around
A dark man in a market place,
Singing to men of his own race,
With long blithe ripples in the sound,
Of isles enchanted, love and wrath,
And of Achilles' deadly path;
The great ash spear he used to fling;
The bow one man alone could string;
Odysseus in the sea immersed
Who never heard of "Safety First,"
Nor went to a Peace Conference:
For Homer was a man of sense,
And knew right well the only themes
Of Song, when men have time for dreams.
And then, indignant, down the lane
The great dark beggar roared again.

ARCHIBALD MacLEISH

You, Andrew Marvell 21

And here face down beneath the sun
And here upon earth's noonward height
To feel the always coming on
The always rising of the night:

To feel creep up the curving east
The earthy chill of dusk and slow
Upon those under lands the vast
And ever climbing shadow grow

And strange at Ecbatan the trees
Take leaf by leaf the evening strange
The flooding dark about their knees
The mountains over Persia change

And now at Kermanshah the gate
Dark empty and the withered grass
And through the twilight now the late
Few travelers in the westward pass

And Baghdad darken and the bridge
Across the silent river gone
And through Arabia the edge
Of evening widen and steal on

And deepen on Palmyra's street
The wheel rut in the ruined stone
And Lebanon fade out and Crete
High through the clouds and overblown

And over Sicily the air
Still flashing with the landward gulls

And loom and slowly disappear
The sails above the shadowy hulls

And Spain go under and the shore
Of Africa the gilded sand
And evening vanish and no more
The low pale light across that land

Nor now the long light on the sea:

And here face downward in the sun
To feel how swift how secretly
The shadow of the night comes on . . .

ALLEN TATE

Aeneas at Washington

I myself saw furious with blood
Neoptolemus, at his side the black Atridae,
Hecuba and the hundred daughters, Priam
Cut down, his filth drenching the holy fires.
In that extremity I bore me well
A true gentleman, valorous in arms,
Disinterested and honorable. Then fled:
That was a time when civilization
Run by the few fell to the many, and
Crashed to the shout of men, the clang of arms:
Cold victualing I seized, I hoisted up
The old man my father upon my back,
In the smoke made by sea for a new world
Saving little—a mind imperishable
If time is, a love of past things tenuous
As the hesitation of receding love.

(To the reduction of uncitied littorals
We brought chiefly the vigor of prophecy
Our hunger breeding calculation
And fixed triumphs)

The thirsty dove I saw
In the glowing fields of Troy, hemp ripening
And tawny corn, the thickening Blue Grass
All lying rich forever in the green sun.
I see all things apart, the towers that men
Contrive I too contrived long, long ago.
Now I demand little. The singular passion
Abides its object and consumes desire
In the circling shadow of its appetite.
There was a time when the young eyes were slow,
Their flame steady beyond the firstling fire,

I stood in the rain, far from home at nightfall
By the Potomac, the great Dome lit the water,
The city my blood had built I knew no more
While the screech-owl whistled his new delight
Consecutively dark.
                                        Stuck in the wet mire
Four thousand leagues from the ninth buried city
I thought of Troy, what we had built her for.

EDWIN MARKHAM

The Third Wonder 25

'Two things,' said Kant, 'fill me with breathless awe:
The starry heavens and the moral law.'
I know a thing more awful and obscure—
The long, long patience of the plundered poor.

AUDREY WURDEMANN

Text 26

Behold this brief hexagonal,
The honey and the honey-cell,
A tower of wax;—a touch, and see
These walls that could sustain a bee
Clinging with clawed and furry feet
Now bend and break and spill their sweet.

Behold, my dear, the dream we saw,
The thing we built without a flaw,
The amber and the agate rime,
The interstitial beat of time,
The microcosmos of our wit,
The sweetness that we sucked from it,
The honeycomb, the holy land
Broken and bleeding in my hand.

Too Much

A Roman had an
artist, a freedman,
contrive a cone—pine-cone
or fir-cone—with holes for a fountain. Placed on
the Prison of St. Angelo, this cone
of the Pompeys which is known

now as the Popes', passed
for art. A huge cast
bronze, dwarfing the peacock
statue in the garden of the Vatican,
it looks like a work of art made to give
to a Pompey, or native

of Thebes. Others could
build, and understood
making colossi and
how to use slaves, and kept crocodiles and put
baboons on the necks of giraffes to pick
fruit, and used serpent magic.

They had their men tie
hippopotami
and bring out dapple dog-
cats to course antelopes, dikdik, and ibex;
or used small eagles. They looked on as theirs,
impallas and onigers,

the wild ostrich herd
with hard feet and bird
necks rearing back in the

dust like a serpent preparing to strike, cranes,
mongooses, storks, anoas, Nile geese;
and there were gardens for these—

combining planes, dates,
limes, and pomegranates,
in avenues—with square
pools of pink flowers, tame fish, and small frogs.
Besides yarns dyed with indigo, and red
cotton, they had a flax which they spun

into fine linen
cordage for yachtsmen.
These people liked small things;
they gave to boys little paired playthings such as
nests of eggs, ichneumon and snake, paddle
and raft, badger and camel;

and made toys for them-
selves: the royal totem;
and toilet-boxes marked
with the contents. Lords and ladies put goose-grease
paint in round bone boxes with pivoting
lid incised with the duck-wing

or reverted duck-
head; kept in a buck
or rhinoceros horn,
the ground horn; and locust oil in stone locusts.
It was a picture with a fine distance;
of drought, and of assistance

in time, from the Nile
rising slowly, while
    the pig-tailed monkey on
    slab-hands, with arched-up slack-slung gait, and the
        brown dandy, looked at the jasmine two-leafed
        twig and bud, cactus-pads, and fig.

Dwarfs here and there, lent
to an evident
    poetry of frog greys,
    duck-egg greens, and egg-plant blues, a fantasy
        and a verisimilitude that were
        right to those with, everywhere,

power over the poor.
The bees' food is your
    food. Those who tended flower-
    beds and stables were like the king's cane in the
        form of a hand, or the folding bedroom
        made for his mother of whom

he was fond. Princes
clad in queens' dresses,
    calla or petunia
    white, that trembled at the edge, and queens in a
        king's underskirt of fine-twilled thread like silk-
        worm gut, as bee-man and milk-

maid, kept divine cows
and bees; limestone brows,
    and gold-foil wings. They made
    basalt serpents and portraits of beetles; the

king gave his name to them and he was named
for them. He feared snakes, and tamed

Pharaoh's rat, the rust-
backed mongoose. No bust
of it was made, but there
was pleasure for the rat. Its restlessness was
its excellence; it was praised for its wit;
and the jerboa, like it,

a small desert rat,
and not famous, that
lives without water, has
happiness. Abroad seeking food, or at home
in its burrow, the Sahara field-mouse
has a shining silver house

of sand. O rest and
joy, the boundless sand,
the stupendous sand-spout,
no water, no palm-trees, no ivory bed,
tiny cactus; but one would not be he
who has nothing but plenty.

Abundance

Africanus meant
the conqueror sent
from Rome. It should mean the
untouched: the sand-brown jumping-rat—free-born;
and the blacks, that choice race with an
elegance ignored by one's ignorance.

Part terrestrial,
and part celestial,
    Jacob saw, cudgel staff
    in claw-hand—steps of air and air angels; his
        friends were the stones. The translucent mistake
        of the desert, does not make

hardship for one who
can rest and then do
    the opposite—launching
    as if on wings, from its match-thin hind legs, in
        daytime or at night; with the tail as a weight,
        undulated by speed, straight.

Looked at by daylight,
the underside's white,
    though the fur on the back
    is buff-brown like the breast of the fawn-breasted
        bower-bird. It hops like the fawn-breast, but has
        chipmunk contours—perceived as

it turns its bird head—
the nap directed
    neatly back and blending
    with the ear which reiterates the slimness
        of the body. The fine hairs on the tail,
        repeating the other pale

markings, lengthen till
at the tip they fill
    out in a tuft—black and
    white; strange detail of the simplified creature,

        fish-shaped and silvered to steel by the force
        of the large desert moon. Course

the jerboa, or
plunder its food store,
    and you will be cursed. It
    honours the sand by assuming its colour;
        closed upper paws seeming one with the fur
        in its flight from a danger.

By fifths and sevenths,
in leaps of two lengths,
    like the uneven notes
    of the Bedouin flute, it stops its gleaning
        on little wheel castors, and makes fern-seed
        foot-prints with kangaroo speed.

Its leaps should be set
to the flageolet;
    pillar body erect
    on a three-cornered smooth-working Chippendale
        claw—propped on hind legs, and tail as third toe,
        between leaps to its burrow.

MURIEL RUKEYSER

Effort at Speech Between Two People 33

: Speak to me. Take my hand. What are you now?
I will tell you all. I will conceal nothing.
When I was three, a little child read a story about a rabbit
who died, in the story, and I crawled under a chair :
a pink rabbit : it was my birthday, and a candle
burnt a sore spot on my finger, and I was told to be happy.

: Oh, grow to know me. I am not happy. I will be open :
Now I am thinking of white sails against a sky like music,
like glad horns blowing, and birds tilting, and an arm about me.
There was one I loved, who wanted to live, sailing.

: Speak to me. Take my hand. What are you now?
When I was nine, I was fruitily sentimental,
fluid : and my widowed aunt played Chopin,
and I bent my head on the painted woodwork, and wept.
I want now to be close to you. I would
link the minutes of my days close, somehow, to your days.

I am not happy. I will be open.
I have liked lamps in evening corners, and quiet poems.

There has been fear in my life. Sometimes I
speculate
On what a tragedy his life was, really.

: Take my hand. Fist my mind in your
hand. What are you now?
When I was fourteen, I had dreams of suicide,
and I stood at a steep window, at sunset, hoping
toward death :
if the light had not melted clouds and plains to
beauty,
if light had not transformed that day, I would have
leapt.
I am unhappy. I am lonely. Speak to me.

: I will be open. I think he never loved me :
he loved the bright beaches, the little lips of foam
that ride small waves, he loved the veer of gulls :
he said with a gay mouth : I love you. Grow to
know me.

: What are you now? If we could touch one
another,
if these our separate entities could come to grips,
clenched like a Chinese puzzle . . . yesterday
I stood in a crowded street that was live with people,
and no one spoke a word, and the morning shone.
Everyone silent, moving. . . . Take my
hand. Speak to me.

CARL SANDBURG

The People, Yes, 11 35

An Englishman in the old days
presented the Empress of Russia
with a life-sized flea made of gold
and it could hop.

She asked the court:
"What can we Russians do
to equal this marvel?"

A minister took it away
and brought it back soon after.
He had seen to it
and had the monogram of the Empress
engraved on each foot of the flea
though it would no longer hop.

This is a case in point
as told by Salzman
who came from the Caucasus
and had it from a man who was there.

In Tiflis, his home town,
Salzman knew a merchant
who stood in the front door
and spoke to passersby,
to possible customers:
    "Come inside.
    We've got everything—
    even bird's milk."

And this merchant weighed his hand
along with what he sold his patrons
and each evening after business hours

he threw holy water on his hand
saying, "Cleanse thyself, cleanse thyself."

Among the peasants Salzman heard:
"He should be the owner of the land
who rubs it between his hands every spring."

Wood rangers in the forest of the czar
came in and talked all night.
They spoke of forest sounds:
"The cry of a virgin tree at its first cut of the ax stays in
the air.
"The sound of the blow that kills a snake is in the air till
sundown.
"The cry of the child wrongfully punished stays in the
air."

And this was in the old days
and they are a fine smoke
a thin smoke.

The people move
in a fine thin smoke,
the people, yes.

DUDLEY FITTS

Ya Se Van Los Pastores

Lady, the shepherds have all gone
To Extremadura, taking their sheep with them,

Their musical instruments also, their singing:
We shall not see them again.

Therefore bring lute, flute, or other melodious machine,
And we shall sit under this plane-tree and perform upon
it.

There is no help for it: use your eyes:

The shepherds, Lady, have gone into Extremadura,
Eastward, into sunrise.

PERCY MacKAYE

After Tempest 38

Shell-less, on your slimey trail,
In mornless dawn, I meet you, snail:
Sans house, sans home, sans bivouac,
No arc of wonder spans your back.

Here, on time's storm-shattered shelf,
Slug, you meet your crawling self,
Reaching towards eternity
All-unavailing antennae!

LEONORA SPEYER

Swans

With wings held close and slim neck bent,
Along dark water scarcely stirred,
Floats, glimmering and indolent,
The alabaster bird;

Floats near its mate—the lovely one!
They lie like snow, cool flake on flake,
Mild breast on breast of dimmer swan
Dim-mirrored in the lake.

They glide—and glides that white embrace,
Shy bird to bird with never a sound;
Thus leaned Narcissus toward his face,
Leaned lower till he drowned.

Leda leaned thus, subdued and spent
Beneath those vivid wings of love;
Along the lake, proud, indolent,
The vast birds scarcely move.

Silence is wisdom. Then how wise
Are these whose song is but their knell!
A god did well to choose this guise.
Truly, a god did well.

my father moved through dooms of love
through sames of am through haves of give,
singing each morning out of each night
my father moved through depths of height

this motionless forgetful where
turned at his glance to shining here;
that if (so timid air is firm)
under his eyes would stir and squirm

newly as from unburied which
floats the first who,his april touch
drove sleeping selves to swarm their fates
woke dreamers to their ghostly roots

and should some why completely weep
my father's fingers brought her sleep:
vainly no smallest voice might cry
for he could feel the mountains grow.

Lifting the valleys of the sea
my father moved through griefs of joy;
praising a forehead called the moon
singing desire into begin

joy was his song and joy so pure
a heart of star by him could steer
and pure so now and now so yes
the wrists of twilight would rejoice

keen as midsummer's keen beyond
conceiving mind of sun will stand,

so strictly (over utmost him
so hugely) stood my father's dream

his flesh was flesh his blood was blood:
no hungry man but wished him food;
no cripple wouldn't creep one mile
uphill to only see him smile.

Scorning the pomp of must and shall
my father moved through dooms of feel;
his anger was as right as rain
his pity was as green as grain

septembering arms of year extend
less humbly wealth to foe and friend
than he to foolish and to wise
offered immeasurable is

proudly and (by octobering flame
beckoned) as earth will downward climb,
so naked for immortal work
his shoulders marched against the dark

his sorrow was as true as bread:
no liar looked him in the head;
if every friend became his foe
he'd laugh and build a world with snow.

My father moved through theys of we,
singing each new leaf out of each tree
(and every child was sure that spring
danced when she heard my father sing)

then let men kill which cannot share,
let blood and flesh be mud and mire,
scheming imagine,passion willed,
freedom a drug that's bought and sold

giving to steal and cruel kind,
a heart to fear,to doubt a mind,
to differ a disease of same,
conform the pinnacle of am

though dull were all we taste as bright,
bitter all utterly things sweet,
maggoty minus and dumb death
all we inherit,all bequeath

and nothing quite so least as truth
—i say though hate were why men breathe—
because my father lived his soul
love is the whole and more than all

MAX EASTMAN

Animal

Could you, so arrantly of earth, so cool,
With coarse harsh hair and rapid agile pace,
So built to beat boys in a swimming race
Or dive with sheer terns to a salty pool,
So lean, so animally beautiful—
Your breasts look sideways like a heifer's face,
And you stand sometimes with a surly grace
And mutinous blue eye-fires like a bull—
Could you from this most envied poise descend,
Moved by some force in me I know not of,
To mix with me and be to me a woman,
Diana down from heaven could not lend
More ecstasy, or fill my faltering human
Heart's hunger with a more celestial love.

JOHN NEIHARDT

From *The Song of Jed Smith* 44

One more rendezvous—
And only silence waiting after all!

The nights were nippy with a tang of Fall
Along the lone road leading to the States—
The season when the dying Summer waits
To listen for the whisper of the snow
A long way off. Three horseback days below
The Arkansaw, and twelve from Santa Fé
I crossed the Cimarrone; another day
Beyond the waterholes, and that was where
He left the wagons.

All around me there
Was empty desert, level as a sea,
And like a picture of eternity
Completed for the holding of regret.
But I could almost see the oxen yet
Droop, panting, in the circled wagon train;
The anxious eyes that followed on the plain
A solitary horseman growing dim;
And, riding south, I almost sighted him
Along the last horizon—many moons
Ahead of me.

Beyond a strip of dunes
I came upon the Cimarrone once more,
A winding flat no wetter than the shore,
Excepting when you clawed a hole, it filled.
But hunting for the spot where he was killed
Was weary work. There had to be a ledge
Of sandstone jutting from the river's edge
Southwestwardly; and, balanced at the tip,

A bowlder, waiting for a flood, to slip
And tumble in the stream; and just below,
Not any farther than a good knife-throw,
A hiding place behind a point of clay.

But there was sand—and sand.

The second day,
When I was sure the Mexicans had sold
The buyer's wish, with twilight getting cold
And blue along a northward bend, I came
Upon it with a start—the very same,
Except the bowlder bedded in the stream!
And like one helpless in an evil dream,
I seemed to see it all. The burning glare,
The pawing horse, and 'Diah clawing there
Beneath the ledge, beyond the reach of sound
To warn him of the faces peering round
The point of clay behind; a sheath-knife thrown,
Bows twanging; 'Diah fighting all alone,
A-bristle with the arrows and the knife—
Alone, alone, and fighting for his life
With twenty yelling devils; left for dead,
The bloody, feathered huddle that was Jed,
Half buried in Comanches, coming to;
The slow red trail, the hard, last trail that grew
Behind him, crawling up the bank to seek
The frightened horse; too dizzy sick and weak
To make it past the sepulcher of shade
The sandstone ledge and balanced bowlder made
Against the swimming dazzle of the sun;
The band returning for the horse and gun
To find him there, still moaning, in his tomb

And roll the bowlder on him.
—*Only gloom*
And silence left!"

The voice of sorrow rose
And ceased. Assenting in a semi-doze,
The elder nodded sagely; and the Squire
Breathed deeper. Feeling by the fallen fire
The mystery of sorrow in the cry,
The dog sat up and, muzzle to the sky,
Mourned for the dear one mourning.

RIDGELY TORRENCE

Adam's Dying

He dreamed first
  Of what seem
The things worst
  In the dream:

The lost bower,
  The grave's drouth,
The sword's power,
  The worm's mouth.

He dreamed last
  Of good things:
The pain past,
  The air's wings.

The seed furled,
  The stirred dust,
Sight's world,
  The hand's thrust.

Thought's birth,
  The mind's blade,
Work's worth,
  The thing made.

The wind's haste,
  The cloud's dove,
The fruit's taste,
  The heart's love.

The sky's dome,
  The sun's west,

A man's home,
  Eve's breast.

The wave's beach,
  The bird's wood,
Dreams, each,
  But all good.

Life finds rest
  Where life rose.
Which was best?
  The heart knows.

He would declare and could himself believe
That the birds there in all the garden round
From having heard the daylong voice of Eve
Had added to their own an oversound,
Her tone of meaning but without the words.
Admittedly an eloquence so soft
Could only have had an influence on birds
When call or laughter carried it aloft.
Be that as may be, she was in their song.
Moreover her voice upon their voices crossed
Had now persisted in the woods so long
That probably it never would be lost.
Never again would birds' song be the same.
And to do that to birds was why she came.

RANDALL JARRELL

90 North 50

At home, in my flannel gown, like a bear to its floe,
I clambered to bed; up the globe's impossible sides
I sailed all night—till at last, with my black beard,
My furs and my dogs, I stood at the northern pole.

There in the childish night my companions lay frozen,
The stiff furs knocked at my starveling throat,
And I gave my great sigh: the flakes came huddling,
Were they really my end? In the darkness I turned to my
    rest.

—Here, the flag snaps in the glare and silence
Of the unbroken ice. I stand here,
The dogs bark, my beard is black, and I stare
At the North Pole . . .
                    And now what? Why, go back.

Turn as I please, my step is to the south.
The world—my world spins on this final point
Of cold and wretchedness: all lines, all winds
End in this whirlpool I at last discover.

And it is meaningless. In the child's bed
After the night's voyage, in that warm world
Where people work and suffer for the end
That crowns the pain—in that Cloud-Cuckoo-Land

I reached my North and it had meaning.
Here at the actual pole of my existence,
Where all that I have done is meaningless,
Where I die or live by accident alone—

Where, living or dying, I am still alone;
Here where North, the night, the berg of death
Crowd me out of the ignorant darkness,
I see at last that all the knowledge

I wrung from the darkness—that the darkness flung me—
Is worthless as ignorance: nothing comes from nothing,
The darkness from the darkness. Pain comes from the
    darkness
And we call it wisdom. It is pain.

LEONARD BACON

Flyfisherman in Wartime 52

Shall I ever see it, the Queen's River
With the Hathaway pitches riffling down?
Or is it lost to me now and for ever,
Where the laurel whitened, the hackle was brown?

Perhaps my grandson may cast his fly
Where the straight bronze current skews at the turn.
Luck to his fishing! Light to his eye!
Strength to his wrist! And the wit to learn!

I was not wise, and my thought was simple,
Quick to be read by a hasty reader.
May he know more, where the eddies dimple,
Than I when I darted the dry-fly leader.

May he know, as I knew, the hard drops pounding
That hammered the black pool silver-white,
Pan's shout through the summer squall resounding,
And the trout that struck in the thunderlight.

RICHARD EBERHART

The Fury of Aerial Bombardment

You would think the fury of aerial bombardment
Would rouse God to relent; the infinite spaces
Are still silent. He looks on shock-pried faces.
History, even, does not know what is meant.

You would feel after so many centuries
God would give man to repent; yet he can kill
As Cain could, but with multitudinous will,
No farther advanced than in his ancient furies.

Was man made stupid to see his own stupidity?
Is God by definition indifferent, beyond us all?
Is the eternal truth man's fighting soul
Wherein the Beast ravens in its own avidity?

Of Van Wettering I speak, and Averill,
Names on a list, whose faces I do not recall
But they are gone to early death, who late in school
Distinguished the belt feed lever from the belt holding
pawl.

KENNETH REXROTH

Strength Through Joy 54

Coming back over the col between
Isosceles Mountain and North Palisade,
I stop at the summit and look back
At the storm gathering over the white peaks
Of the Whitney group and the colored
Kaweahs. September, nineteen-thirty-nine.
This is the last trip in the mountains
This autumn, possibly the last trip ever.
The storm clouds rise up the mountainside,
Lightning batters the pinnacles above me,
The clouds beneath the pass are purple
And I see rising through them from the valleys
And cities a cold, murderous flood,
Spreading over the world, lapping at the last
Inviolate heights; mud streaked yellow
With gas, slimy and blotched with crimson,
Filled with broken bits of steel and flesh,
Moving slowly with the blind motion
Of lice, spreading inexorably
As bacteria spread in tissues,
Swirling with the precise rapacity of starved rats.
I loiter here like a condemned man
Lingers over his last breakfast, his last smoke;
Thinking of those heroes of the war
Of human skill, foresight, endurance and will;
The disinterested bravery,
The ideal combat of peace: Bauer
Crawling all night around his icecave
On snowbound Kanchenjunga, Tilman
And Shipton skylarking on Nanda Devi,
Smythe seeing visions on Everest,
The mad children of the Eigerwand—
What holidays will they keep this year?

Gun emplacements blasted in the rock;
No place for graves, the dead covered with quicklime
Or left in the snow till the spring thaw;
Machine gun duels between white robed ski troops,
The last screaming schusses marked with blood.
Was it for this we spent the years perfecting
The craft of courage? Better the corpse
Of the foolhardy, frozen on the Eiger
Accessible only to the storm,
Standing sentry for the avalanche.

JESSE STUART

Speaks the Whispering Grass

See young John Sutton with his Kathaleen
In love with life, alive to kiss and dreams;
A fairer couple I have never seen
Through April eyes of my green liquid stems!
Now let them love while spring is in their blood,
Know joy of living, ecstasy, and pain;
And let them know each coming season's mood,
Let them know life that will not come again.

Snakes, lizards, scorpions, boast eternal spring
But I shall drink their cold blood through my tendrils;
Fair Kathaleen and John who laugh and sing
Will give to me their portion for my petals!
Even, slow shell-protected terrapin
Shall give my fibers strength, bone for my stems;
I nurture everything but blowing wind,
The lamps of Heaven and earth's buried dreams.

MARK VAN DOREN

The Seven Sleepers

The liberal arts lie eastward of this shore.
Choppy the waves at first. Then the long swells
And the being lost. Oh, centuries of salt
Till the surf booms again, and comes more land.

Not even there, except that old men point
At passes up the mountains. Over which,
Oh, centuries of soil, with olive trees
For twisted shade, and helicons for sound.

Then eastward seas, boned with peninsulas.
Then, orient, the islands; and at last,
The cave, the seven sleepers. Who will rise
And sing to you in numbers till you know

White magic. Which remember. Do you hear?
Oh, universe of sand that you must cross,
And animal the night. But do not rest.
The centuries are stars, and stud the way.

W. H. AUDEN

In Praise of Limestone 58

If it form the one landscape that we the inconstant ones
Are consistently homesick for, this is chiefly
Because it dissolves in water. Mark these rounded slopes
With their surface fragrance of thyme and beneath
A secret system of caves and conduits; hear these springs
That spurt out everywhere with a chuckle
Each filling a private pool for its fish and carving
Its own little ravine whose cliffs entertain
The butterfly and the lizard; examine this region
Of short distances and definite places:
What could be more like Mother or a fitter background
For her son, for the nude young male who lounges
Against a rock displaying his dildo, never doubting
That for all his faults he is loved, whose works are but
Extensions of his power to charm? From weathered outcrop
To hill-top temple, from appearing waters to
Conspicuous fountains, from a wild to a formal vineyard,
Are ingenious but short steps that a child's wish
To receive more attention than his brothers, whether
By pleasing or teasing, can easily take.

Watch, then, the band of rivals as they climb up and down
Their steep stone gennels in twos and threes, sometimes
Arm in arm, but never, thank God, in step; or engaged
On the shady side of a square at midday in
Voluble discourse, knowing each other too well to think
There are any important secrets, unable
To conceive a god whose temper-tantrums are moral
And not to be pacified by a clever line
Or a good lay: for, accustomed to a stone that responds,

They have never had to veil their faces in awe
Of a crater whose blazing fury could not be fixed;
Adjusted to the local needs of valleys

Where everything can be touched or reached by walking,
Their eyes have never looked into infinite space
Through the lattice-work of a nomad's comb; born lucky,
Their legs have never encountered the fungi
And insects of the jungle, the monstrous forms and lives
With which we have nothing, we like to hope, in
common.
So, when one of them goes to the bad, the way his mind
works
Remains comprehensible: to become a pimp
Or deal in fake jewelry or ruin a fine tenor voice
For effects that bring down the house could happen to
all
But the best and the worst of us . . .
That is why, I suppose,
The best and worst never stayed here long but sought
Immoderate soils where the beauty was not so external,
The light less public and the meaning of life
Something more than a mad camp. "Come!" cried the
granite wastes,
"How evasive is your humor, how accidental
Your kindest kiss, how permanent is death." (Saints-to-be
Slipped away sighing.) "Come!" purred the clays and
gravels,
"On our plains there is room for armies to drill; rivers
Wait to be tamed and slaves to construct you a tomb
In the grand manner: soft as the earth is mankind and
both
Need to be altered." (Intendant Caesars rose and

Left, slamming the door.) But the really reckless were fetched
By an older colder voice, the oceanic whisper:
"I am the solitude that asks and promises nothing;
That is how I shall set you free. There is no love;
There are only the various envies, all of them sad."
They were right, my dear, all those voices were right
And still are; this land is not the sweet home that it looks,
Nor its peace the historical calm of a site
Where something was settled once and for all: A backward
And dilapidated province, connected
To the big busy world by a tunnel, with a certain
Seedy appeal, is that all it is now? Not quite:
It has a worldly duty which in spite of itself
It does not neglect, but calls into question
All the Great Powers assume; it disturbs our rights. The poet,
Admired for his earnest habit of calling
The sun the sun, his mind Puzzle, is made uneasy
By these solid statues which so obviously doubt
His antimythological myth; and these gamins,
Pursuing the scientist down the tiled colonnade
With such lively offers, rebuke his concern for Nature's
Remotest aspects: I, too, am reproached, for what
And how much you know. Not to lose time, not to get caught,
Not to be left behind, not, please! to resemble

The beasts who repeat themselves, or a thing like water
Or stone whose conduct can be predicted, these

Are our Common Prayer, whose greatest comfort is music
  Which can be made anywhere, is invisible,
And does not smell. In so far as we have to look forward
  To death as a fact, no doubt we are right: But if
Sins can be forgiven, if bodies rise from the dead,
  These modifications of matter into
Innocent athletes and gesticulating fountains,
  Made solely for pleasure, make a further point:
The blessed will not care what angle they are regarded
    from,
  Having nothing to hide. Dear, I know nothing of
Either, but when I try to imagine a faultless love
  Or the life to come, what I hear is the murmur
Of underground streams, what I see is a limestone
    landscape.

ROLFE HUMPHRIES

The Offering of the Heart 62
Tapestry from Arras, XV Century

Against a somber background, blue as midnight,
More blank and dark than cloud, as black as storm,
The almost moving leaves are almost golden,
The light is almost warm.

Seated, a lady, wearing a cloak with ermine
Holds on her hand, correctly gloved and bent,
A falcon, without feathered hood or jesses;
Her gaze appears intent

On what her hound, good little dog, is doing
Around her ankles, left front paw in air,
Regardless of the three white careless rabbits—
He does not see them there,

Or turn, as does the falcon, toward the gallant,
The gentleman, more elegant than smart,
Who comes, in crimson cloak with ermine lining,
And offers her a heart,

Holding it, chastely, between thumb and finger
Whose U it does not fill, a plum in size,
A somewhat faded strawberry in color—
She does not raise her eyes.

How can a heart be beating in the bosom,
And yet held up, so tiny, in the hand?
Innocence; mystery: an Age of Science
Would hardly understand.

ROBERT FRANCIS

Squash in Blossom 63

How lush, how loose, the uninhibited squash is.
If ever hearts (and these immoderate leaves
Are vegetable hearts) were worn on sleeves,
The squash's are. In green the squash vine gushes.

The flowers are cornucopias of summer,
Briefly exuberant and cheaply golden.
And if they make a show of being hidden,
Are open promiscuously to every comer.

Let the squash be what it was doomed to be
By the old Gardener with the shrewd green thumb.
Let it expand and sprawl, defenceless, dumb.
But let me be the fiber-disciplined tree

Whose leaf (with something to say in wind) is small,
Reduced to the ingenuity of a green splinter
Sharp to defy or fraternize with winter,
Or if not that, prepared in fall to fall.

ROBERT NATHAN

Now Blue October 64

Now blue October, smoky in the sun,
Must end the long, sweet summer of the heart.
The last brief visit of the birds is done;
They sing the autumn songs before they part.
Listen, how lovely—there's the thrush we heard
When June was small with roses, and the bending
Blossom of branches covered nest and bird,
Singing the summer in, summer unending—
Give me your hand once more before the night;
See how the meadows darken with the frost,
How fades the green that was the summer's light.
Beauty is only altered, never lost,
And love, before the cold November rain,
Will make its summer in the heart again.

The free evening fades, outside the windows fastened
with decorative iron grilles.
The lamps are lighted; the shades drawn; the nurses are
watching a little.
It is the hour of the complicated knitting on the safe
bone needles; of the games of anagrams and bridge;
The deadly game of chess; the book held up like a mask.

The period of the wildest weeping, the fiercest delusion,
is over.
The women rest their tired half-healed hearts; they are
almost well.
Some of them will stay almost well always: the blunt-
faced woman whose thinking dissolved
Under academic discipline; the manic depressive girl
Now leveling off; one paranoiac afflicted with jealousy.
Another with persecution. Some alleviation has been
possible.

O fortunate bride, who never again will become elated
after childbirth!
O lucky older wife, who has been cured of feeling
unwanted!
To the suburban railway station you will return, return,
To meet forever Jim home on the 5:35.
You will be again as normal and selfish and heartless as
anybody else.

There is life left: the piano says it with its octave smile.
The soft carpets pad the thump and splinter of the
suicide to be.
Everything will be splendid: the grandmother will not
drink habitually.

The fruit salad will bloom on the plate like a bouquet
And the garden produce the blue-ribbon aquilegia.

The cats will be glad; the fathers feel justified; the
mothers relieved.
The sons and husbands will no longer need to pay the
bills.
Childhoods will be put away, the obscene nightmare
abated.

At the ends of the corridors the baths are running.
Mrs. C. again feels the shadow of the obsessive idea.
Miss R. looks at the mantel-piece, which must mean
something.

Cigar Smoke, Sunday, After Dinner

Smell of cigar smoke, Sunday, after dinner,
Our eyes upon the visitor, leaning back
From robust lengthy elegance of dining,
White fingers catching up the golden slack
Of watch chain slung across expansive chest,
Rippling the links into a silken banner. . . .
All else was solid, black and white and shining,
The polished shirt-front and the black mustache,
Even the smooth fine broadcloth of the vest
Shone with a dark and unaccustomed luster.

Save that the damask throws a burnished flash,
The room, the coffee and the talk, are lost;
Only lives on the one compelling cluster,
The composition masterfully glossed,
Portrait of manhood and its ease of manner,
Rich as cigar smoke after Sunday dinner,
And how the white hand flicked away the ash.

LÉONIE ADAMS

Grapes Making 68

Noon sun beats down the leaf; the noon
Of summer burns along the vine
And thins the leaf with burning air,
Till from the underleaf is fanned,
And down the woven vine, the light.
Still the pleached leaves drop layer on layer
To wind the sun on either hand,
And echoes of the light are bound,
And hushed the blazing cheek of light,
The hurry of the breathless noon,
And from the thicket of the vine
The grape has pressed into its round.

The grape has pressed into its round,
And swings, aloof chill green, clean won
Of light, between the sky and ground;
Those hid, soft-flashing lamps yet blind,
Which yield an apprehended sun.
Fresh triumph in a courteous kind,
Having more ways to be, and years,
And easy, countless treasuries,
You whose all-told is still no sum,
Like a rich heart, well-said in sighs,
The careless autumn mornings come,
The grapes drop glimmering to the shears.

Now shady sod at heel piles deep,
An overarching shade, the vine
Across the fall of noon is flung;
And here beneath the leaves is cast
A light to colour noonday sleep,
While cool, bemused the grape is swung
Beneath the eyelids of the vine;

And deepening like a tender thought
Green moves along the leaf, and bright
The leaf above, and leaf has caught,
And emerald pierces day, and last
The faint leaf vanishes to light.

WILLIAM CARLOS WILLIAMS

The Mental Hospital Garden 70

It is far to Assisi,
but not too far:
Over this garden,
brooding over this garden,
there is a kindly spirit,
brother to the poor
and who is poorer than he
who is in love
when birds are nesting
in the spring of the year?
They came
to eat from his hand
who had nothing,
and yet
from his plenty
he fed them all.
All mankind
grew to be his debtors,
a simple story.
Love is in season.
At such a time,
hyacinth time
in
the hospital garden,
the time
of the coral-flowered
and early salmon-pink
clusters, it is
the time also of
abandoned birds' nests
before
the sparrows start
to tear them apart

against the advent of that bounty
from which
they will build anew.
All about them
on the lawns
the young couples
embrace
as in a tale
by Boccaccio.
They are careless
under license of the disease
which has restricted them
to these grounds.
St. Francis forgive them
and all lovers
whoever they may be.
They have seen
a great light, it
springs from their own bawdy foreheads.
The light
is sequestered there
by these enclosing walls.
They are divided
from their fellows.
It is a bounty
from a last year's bird's nest.
St. Francis,
who befriended the wild birds,
by their aid,
those who
have nothing
and live
by the Holy light of love

that rules,
blocking despair,
over this garden.
Time passes.
The pace has slackened
But with the falling off
of the pace
the scene has altered.
The lovers raise their heads,
at that which has come over them.
It is summer now.
The broad sun
shines!
Blinded by the light
they walk bewildered,
seeking
between the leaves
for a vantage
from which to view
the advancing season.
They are incredulous
of their own cure
and half minded
to escape
into the dark again.
The scene
indeed has changed.
By St. Francis
the whole scene
has changed.
They glimpse
a surrounding sky
and the whole countryside.

Filled with terror
    they seek
        a familiar flower
at which to warm themselves,
    but the whole field
        accosts them.
They hide their eyes
    ashamed
        before that bounty,
peering through their fingers
    timidly.
        The saint is watching,
his eyes filled with pity.
The year is still young
    but not so young
        as they
who face the fears
    with which
        they are confronted.
Reawakened
    after love's first folly
        they resemble children
roused from a long sleep.
    Summer is here,
        right enough.
The saint
    has tactfully withdrawn.
        One
emboldened,
    parting the leaves before her,
        stands in the full sunlight,
alone
    shading her eyes

as her heart
beats wildly
and her mind
drinks up
the full meaning
of it
all!

It is Leviathan, mountain and world,
Yet in its grandeur we perceive
This flutter of the impalpable arriving
Like moths and heartbeats, flakes of snow
Falling on wool, or clouds of thought
Trailing rain in the mind: some old one's dream
Of hauling canvas, or the joy of swording
Hard rascals with a smack—for lordly blood
Circulates tenderly and will seep away;
And the winds blowing across the day
From quarters numberless, going where words go
And songs go, even the holy songs, or where
Leaves, showering, go with the spindling grasses.
Into this mountain shade everything passes.
The slave lays down his bones here and the hero,
Thrown, goes reeling with blinded face;
The long desired opens her scorched armpits.
A mountain; so a gloom and air of ghosts,
But charged with utter light if this is light,
A feathery mass, where this beholding
Shines among lustrous fiddles and codices,
Or dusky angels painted against gold
With lutes across their knees. Magical grain
Bound up in splay sheaves on an evening field,
And a bawling calf butchered—these feed
The curious coil of man. A man, this man,
Bred among lakes and railway cars and smoke,
The salt of childhood on his wintry lips,
His full heart ebbing toward the new tide
Arriving, arriving, in laughter and cries,
Down the chaotic dawn and eastern drift,
Would hail the unforeseen, and celebrate
On the great mountainside those sprites,

Tongues of delight, that may remember him—
The yet unborn, trembling in the same rooms,
Breakfasting before the same grey windows,
Lying, grieving again; yet all beyond him,
Who knew he lived in rough Jehovah's breath,
And burned, a quiet wick in a wild night,
Loving what he beheld and will behold.

What had November done?
It wore its trees at breast like English swans
on the green swell triumphant and immortal
through spring and summer: so seeing them
from the edge, caught one's breath, to have discovered

perfection in a long single line, dawn to dusk.

But was it threats and mutters of the envious dead
infected, frightened them, that they arose
an immense fleet sailing the autumn storm
fleeing before dawn?
Shadow of those wings
fell in blight on the acres, turned their choral surf
to a hoarse whisper through a common sedge.

And where each swan rode like a king to throne: only
a bony ghost the contemptuous wind makes light of.

BABETTE DEUTSCH

Earliness at the Cape 78

The color of silence is the oyster's color
Between the lustres of deep night and dawn.
Earth turns to absence; the sole shape's the sleeping
Light—a mollusk of mist. Remote,
A sandspit hinges the valves of that soft monster
Yawning at Portugal. Alone wakeful, lanterns
Over a dark hull to eastward mark
The tough long pull, hidden, the killing
Work, hidden, to feed a hidden world.
Muteness is all. Even the greed of the gulls
Annulled, the hush of color everywhere
The hush of motion. This is the neap of the blood,
Of memory, thought, desire; if pain visits
Such placelessness, it has phantom feet.
What's physical is lost here in ignorance
Of its own being. That solitary boat,
Out fishing, is a black stroke on vacancy.
Night, deaf and dumb as something from the deeps,
Having swallowed whole bright yesterday, replete
With radiance, is gray as abstinence now.
But in this nothingness, a knife point: pleasure
Comes pricking; the hour's pallor, too, is bladed
Like a shell, and as it opens, cuts.

If the deep wood is haunted, it is I
Who am the ghost; not the tall trees
Nor the white moonlight slanting down like rain,
Filling the hollows with bright pools of silver.

A long train whistle serpentines around the hill
Now shrill, now far away.
Tell me, from what dark smoky terminal
What train sets out for yesterday?

Or, since our spirits take off and resume
Their flesh as travellers their cloaks, O tell me where,
In what age and what country you will come,
That I may meet you there.

NED O'GORMAN

The Kiss

Talk of passion is a winter thing,
a huddle of girls, descending wind.
There is no vehicle in a kiss
to carry fury and originality.
In that wherewithal of mouth
the body greets with cannon
the profundis and halt clamavi
of the virgin. Dying is a kiss,
it has broken me. It rimes with tiger
and the gallow tree.

When you come, as you soon must, to the streets of our
    city,
Mad-eyed from stating the obvious,
Not proclaiming our fall but begging us
In God's name to have self-pity,

Spare us all word of the weapons, their force and range,
The long numbers that rocket the mind;
Our slow, unreckoning hearts will be left behind,
Unable to fear what is too strange.

Nor shall you scare us with talk of the death of the race.
How should we dream of this place without us?—
The sun mere fire, the leaves untroubled about us,
A stone look on the stone's face?

Speak of the world's own change. Though we cannot
    conceive
Of an undreamt thing, we know to our cost
How the dreamt cloud crumbles, the vines are blackened
    by frost,
How the view alters. We could believe,

If you told us so, that the white-tailed deer will slip
Into perfect shade, grown perfectly shy,
The lark avoid the reaches of our eye,
The jack-pine lose its knuckled grip

On the cold ledge, and every torrent burn
As Xanthus once, its gliding trout
Stunned in a twinkling. What should we be without
The dolphin's arc, the dove's return,

These things in which we have seen ourselves and
spoken?
Ask us, prophet, how we shall call
Our natures forth when that live tongue is all
Dispelled, that glass obscured or broken

In which we have said the rose of our love and the clean
Horse of our courage, in which beheld
The singing locust of the soul unshelled,
And all we mean or wish to mean.

Ask us, ask us whether with the worldless rose
Our hearts shall fail us; come demanding
Whether there shall be lofty or long standing
When the bronze annals of the oak-tree close.

X. J. KENNEDY

In a Prominent Bar in Secaucus One Day 83

To the tune of "The Old Orange Flute"
or the tune of "Sweet Betsy from Pike"

In a prominent bar in Secaucus one day
Rose a lady in skunk with a topheavy sway,
Raised a knobby red finger—all turned from their beer—
While with eyes bright as snowcrust she sang high and
    clear:

'Now who of you'd think from an eyeload of me
That I once was a lady as proud as could be?
Oh I'd never sit down by a tumbledown drunk
If it wasn't, my dears, for the high cost of junk.

'All the gents used to swear that the white of my calf
Beat the down of the swan by a length and a half.
In the kerchief of linen I caught to my nose
Ah, there never fell snot, but a little gold rose.

'I had seven gold teeth and a toothpick of gold,
My Virginia cheroot was a leaf of it rolled
And I'd light it each time with a thousand in cash—
Why the bums used to fight if I flicked them an ash.

'Once the toast of the Biltmore, the belle of the Taft,
I would drink bottle beer at the Drake, never draft,
And dine at the Astor on Salisbury steak
With a clean tablecloth for each bite I did take.

'In a car like the Roxy I'd roll to the track,
A steel-guitar trio, a bar in the back,
And the wheels made no noise, they turned over so fast,
Still it took you ten minutes to see me go past.

'When the horses bowed down to me that I might
choose,
I bet on them all, for I hated to lose.
Now I'm saddled each night for my butter and eggs
And the broken threads race down the backs of my legs.

'Let you hold in mind, girls, that your beauty must pass
Like a lovely white clover that rusts with its grass.
Keep your bottoms off barstools and marry you young
Or be left—an old barrel with many a bung.

'For when time takes you out for a spin in his car
You'll be hard-pressed to stop him from going too far
And be left by the roadside, for all your good deeds,
Two toadstools for tits and a face full of weeds.'

All the house raised a cheer, but the man at the bar
Made a phonecall and up pulled a red patrol car
And she blew us a kiss as they copped her away
From that prominent bar in Secaucus, N.J.

JOHN HALL WHEELOCK

Hippopotamothalamium

A hippopotamus had a bride
    Of rather singular beauty,
When he lay down at her side
    'Twas out of love, not duty—
    Hers was an exceptional beauty.
Take, oh take those lips away, etc.

He met her in Central Nigeria,
    While she was resident there,
Where life is distinctly superior
    And a hippo can take down her hair—
    And, God, but she was fair!
Take, oh take those lips away, etc.

She was coming up from her morning swim
    When first they chanced to meet:
He looked at her, she looked at him,
    And stood with reluctant feet
    Where mud and river meet.
Take, oh take those lips away, etc.

Their eye-beams, twisted on one thread,
    Instantaneously did twine,
And he made up poetry out of his head,
    Such as: "Dear heart, be mine"—
    And he quoted, line for line,
"*Hail to thee, blithe spirit*", etc.

Now, hippopotamoid courtesy
    Is strangely meticulous—
A beautiful thing, you will agree,
    In a hippopotamus—

And she answered, briefly, thus:
"Hail to thee, blithe spirit", etc.

Perhaps she was practising the arts
That grace old Hippo's daughter,
The coquetries that win all hearts,
For, even as he besought her,
She slid into the water.
Out, out, brief candle, etc.

Now, on the borders of the wood,
Whence love had drawn him hither,
He paces in an anguished mood,
Darting hither and thither
In a terrific dither.
Out, out, brief candle, etc.

The course of true love never yet
Ran smooth, so we are told,
With thorns its pathway is beset
And perils manifold,
So was it from of old.
Out, out, brief candle, etc.

Yet soon a happier morning smiles,
The marriage feast is spread—
The flower girls were crocodiles,
When hippopotamus led
Hippopotamus, with firm tread,
A bride to the bridal bed.
Milton, thou should'st be living at this hour.

JOHN UPDIKE

Telephone Poles

They have been with us a long time.
They will outlast the elms.
Our eyes, like the eyes of a savage sieving the trees
In his search for game,
Run through them. They blend along small-town streets
Like a race of giants that have faded into mere mythology.
Our eyes, washed clean of belief,
Lift incredulous to their fearsome crowns of bolts, trusses, struts, nuts, insulators, and such
Barnacles as compose
These weathered encrustations of electrical debris—
Each a Gorgon's head, which, seized right,
Could stun us to stone.

Yet they are ours. We made them.
See here, where the cleats of linemen
Have roughened a second bark
Onto the bald trunk. And these spikes
Have been driven sideways at intervals handy for human legs.
The Nature of our construction is in every way
A better fit than the Nature it displaces.
What other tree can you climb where the birds' twitter,
Unscrambled, is English? True, their thin shade is negligible,
But then again there is not that tragic autumnal
Casting-off of leaves to outface annually.
These giants are more constant than evergreens
By being never green.

JOHN BERRYMAN

Dream Song #48

He yelled at me in Greek,
my God!—It's not his language
and I'm no good at—his is Aramaic,
was—I am a monoglot of English
(American version) and, say pieces from
a baker's dozen others: where's the bread?

but rising in the Second Gospel, pal:
The seed goes down, god dies.
a rising happens,
some crust, and then occurs   an eating. He said so,
a Greek idea,
troublesome to imaginary Jews,

like bitter Henry, full of the death of love,
Cawdor-uneasy, disambitious, mourning
the whole implausible necessary thing.
He dropped his voice & sybilled of
the death of the death of love.
I óught to get going.

ROBERT LOWELL

For the Union Dead 89

"Relinquunt omnia servare rem publicam."

The old South Boston Aquarium stands
in a Sahara of snow now. Its broken windows are
boarded.
The bronze weathervane cod has lost half its scales.
The airy tanks are dry.

Once my nose crawled like a snail on the glass;
my hand tingled
to burst the bubbles
drifting from the noses of the cowed, compliant fish.

My hand draws back. I often sigh still
for the dark downward and vegetating kingdom
of the fish and reptile. One morning last March,
I pressed against the new barbed and galvanized

fence on the Boston Common. Behind their cage,
yellow dinosaur steamshovels were grunting
as they cropped up tons of mush and grass
to gouge their underworld garage.

Parking spaces luxuriate like civic
sandpiles in the heart of Boston.
A girdle of orange, Puritan-pumpkin colored girders
braces the tingling Statehouse,

shaking over the excavations, as it faces Colonel Shaw
and his bell-cheeked Negro infantry
on St. Gaudens' shaking Civil War relief,
propped by a plank splint against the garage's earthquake.

Two months after marching through Boston,
half the regiment was dead;
at the dedication,
William James could almost hear the bronze Negroes
    breathe.

Their monument sticks like a fishbone
in the city's throat.
Its Colonel is as lean
as a compass-needle.

He has an angry wrenlike vigilance,
a greyhound's gentle tautness;
he seems to wince at pleasure,
and suffocate for privacy.

He is out of bounds now. He rejoices in man's lovely,
peculiar power to choose life and death—
when he leads his black soldiers to death,
he cannot bend his back.

On a thousand small town New England greens,
the old white churches hold their air
of sparse, sincere rebellion; frayed flags
quilt the graveyards of the Grand Army of the Republic.

The stone statues of the abstract Union Soldier
grow slimmer and younger each year—
wasp-wasted, they doze over muskets
and muse through their sideburns . . .

Shaw's father wanted no monument
except the ditch,

where his son's body was thrown
and lost with his "niggers."

The ditch is nearer.
There are no statues for the last war here;
on Boyleston Street, a commercial photograph
shows Hiroshima boiling

over a Mosler Safe, the "Rock of Ages"
that survived the blast. Space is nearer.
When I crouch to my television set,
the drained faces of Negro school-children rise like
    balloons.

Colonel Shaw
is riding on his bubble,
he waits
for the blessèd break.

The Aquarium is gone. Everywhere,
giant finned cars nose forward like fish;
a savage servility
slides by on grease.

ADRIEN STOUTENBERG

Ants and Others 92

Their spare, fanatic sentry comes
across the miles of afternoon
and finds us out, our single crumb
left dozing in a yellowed spoon;
sets up his wireless, reports
to Brown Shirts, comrades, pantry thieves.
(Their army goes like coffee grounds
down doorknobs, drains, up balconies
we meant to guard from minor lusts,
but lacked the key or missed the time.)
Defenseless now the last crust leans
beside a cup. The brown knots climb,
as neat as clocks. I feel the heat
of other lives, and hungers bent
on honeycombs that are not there,
and do not ask what sweet is meant
for which of us, there being such need
of loaves and fishes everywhere.

DAVID WAGONER

The Shooting of John Dillinger Outside the Biograph Theater, July 22, 1934 93

Chicago ran a fever of a hundred and one that groggy Sunday.
A reporter fried an egg on a sidewalk; the air looked shaky.
And a hundred thousand people were in the lake like shirts in a laundry.
Why was Johnny lonely?
Not because two dozen solid citizens, heat-struck, had keeled over backward.
Not because those lawful souls had fallen out of their sockets and melted.
But because the sun went down like a lump in a furnace or a bull in the Stockyards.
Where was Johnny headed?
Under the Biograph Theater sign that said, "Our Air is Refrigerated."
Past seventeen FBI men and four policemen who stood in doorways and sweated.
Johnny sat down in a cold seat to watch Clark Gable get electrocuted.
Had Johnny been mistreated?
Yes, but Gable told the D.A. he'd rather fry than be shut up forever.
Two women sat by Johnny. One looked sweet, one looked like J. Edgar Hoover.
Polly Hamilton made him feel hot, but Anna Sage made him shiver.
Was Johnny a good lover?
Yes, but he passed out his share of squeezes and pokes like a jittery masher
While Agent Purvis sneaked up and down the aisle like an extra usher,

Trying to make sure they wouldn't slip out till the show was over.
Was Johnny a fourflusher?
No, not if he knew the game. He got it up or got it back.
But he liked to take snapshots of policemen with his own Kodak,
And once in a while he liked to take them with an automatic.
Why was Johnny frantic?
Because he couldn't take a walk or sit down in a movie
Without being afraid he'd run smack into somebody
Who'd point at his rearranged face and holler, "Johnny!"
Was Johnny ugly?
Yes, because Dr. Wilhelm Loeser had given him a new profile
With a baggy jawline and squint eyes and an erased dimple,
With kangaroo-tendon cheekbones and a gigolo's mustache that should've been illegal.
Did Johnny love a girl?
Yes, a good-looking, hard-headed Indian named Billie Frechette.
He wanted to marry her and lie down and try to get over it,
But she was locked in jail for giving him first-aid and comfort.
Did Johnny feel hurt?
He felt like breaking a bank or jumping over a railing
Into some panicky teller's cage to shout, "Reach for the ceiling!"
Or like kicking some vice president in the bum checks and smiling.

What was he really doing?
Going up the aisle with the crowd and into the lobby
With Polly saying, "Would *you* do what Clark done?" And Johnny saying, "Maybe."
And Anna saying, "If he'd been smart, he'd of acted like Bing Crosby."
Did Johnny look flashy?
Yes, his white-on-white shirt and tie were luminous.
His trousers were creased like knives to the tops of his shoes,
And his yellow straw hat came down to his dark glasses.
Was Johnny suspicious?
Yes, and when Agent Purvis signalled with a trembling cigar,
Johnny ducked left and ran out of the theater,
And innocent Polly and squealing Anna were left nowhere.
Was Johnny a fast runner?
No, but he crouched and scurried past a friendly liquor store
Under the coupled arms of double-daters, under awnings, under stars,
To the curb at the mouth of an alley. He hunched there.
Was Johnny a thinker?
No, but he was thinking more or less of Billie Frechette
Who was lost in prison for longer than he could possibly wait,
And then it was suddenly too hard to think around a bullet.
Did anyone shoot straight?
Yes, but Mrs. Etta Natalsky fell out from under her picture hat.

Theresa Paulus sprawled on the sidewalk, clutching her left foot.
And both of them groaned loud and long under the streetlight.
Did Johnny like that?
No, but he lay down with those strange women, his face in the alley,
One shoe off, cinders in his mouth, his eyelids heavy.
When they shouted questions at him, he talked back to nobody.
Did Johnny lie easy?
Yes, holding his gun and holding his breath as a last trick,
He waited, but when the Agents came close, his breath wouldn't work.
Clark Gable walked his last mile; Johnny ran half a block.
Did he run out of luck?
Yes, before he was cool, they had him spread out on dished-in marble
In the Cook County Morgue, surrounded by babbling people
With a crime reporter presiding over the head of the table.
Did Johnny have a soul?
Yes, and it was climbing his slippery wind-pipe like a trapped burglar.
It was beating the inside of his ribcage, hollering, "Let me out of here!"
Maybe it got out, and maybe it just stayed there.
Was Johnny a money-maker?
Yes, and thousands paid 25¢ to see him, mostly women,

And one said, "I wouldn't have come, except he's a moral
lesson,"
And another, "I'm disappointed. He feels like a dead
man."
Did Johnny have a brain?
Yes, and it always worked best through the worst of
dangers,
Through flat-footed hammerlocks, through guarded doors,
around corners,
But it got taken out in the morgue and sold to some
doctors.
Could Johnny take orders?
No, but he stayed in the wicker basket carried by six
men
Through the bulging crowd to the hearse and let himself
be locked in,
And he stayed put as it went driving south in a driving
rain.
And he didn't get stolen?
No, not even after his old hard-nosed dad refused to sell
The quick-drawing corpse for $10,000 to somebody in a
carnival.
He figured he'd let *Johnny* decide how to get to Hell.
Did anyone wish him well?
Yes, half of Indiana camped in the family pasture,
And the minister said, "With luck, he could have been a
minister."
And up the sleeve of his oversized gray suit, Johnny
twitched a finger.
Does anyone remember?
Everyone still alive. And some dead ones. It was a new
kind of holiday

With hot and cold drinks and hot and cold tears. They
planted him in a cemetery
With three unknown vice presidents, Benjamin Harrison,
and James Whitcomb Riley,
Who never held up anybody.

Bus Stop

Lights are burning
In quiet rooms
Where lives go on
Resembling ours.

The quiet lives
That follow us—
These lives we lead
But do not own—

Stand in the rain
So quietly
When we are gone,
So quietly . . .

And the last bus
Comes letting dark
Umbrellas out—
Black flowers, black flowers.

And lives go on.
And lives go on
Like sudden lights
At street corners

Or like the lights
In quiet rooms
Left on for hours,
Burning, burning.

Their scrape and clink together of musical coin.
Than the tinkling of crickets more eerie, more thin.
Their click as of crystal, wood, carapace and bone.

A tintinabular fusion. The friction spinal and chill
as of ivory embryo fragments of horn
honed to whistles and flutes.

Windy Eustachian coils cold as the sea,
until held, then warm as the palm.
And snuggled naturally there, smoother than skin.

The curve and continuous spiral, intrinsic. Their role
eternal inversion. Closed
the undulant scroll.

Even when corrugate, sharpness rubbed from their forms,
licked by the mouth of the sea
to tactile charms.

Some blanched by the eye of the sun, a pumice shine
buffing their calcareous nakedness
clean as a tooth.

Some colored like flesh, yet more subtle than corpuscle
dyes.
Some sunsets, some buttermilk skies,
or penumbras of moons in eclipse.

Malachite greens, fish-eyed icy blues,
pigeon-foot pinks, brindled fulvous browns.
Some black, like tektites.

Gathered here in a bowl, their ineradicable inks
vivid, declarative under water,
peculiar fossil-fruits.

They suck through ribbed lips and gaping sutures
into secret clefts
the sweet wet with a tame taste.

Vulviform creatures,
or rather their rocklike backs,
with labial bellies.

Some earhole-shaped,
or funnels with an overlap. Some stony worms
curled up and glazed, the egress like a trumpet.

Some cones, tight twisted sphincters
rugose and spiculate, cactus humped, or warted.
Others slick and simple pods where tender jellies hid.

The rigid souls, the amorphous ones
emptied from out their skeletons
that were their furled caves.

Each an eccentric mummy-case,
one facet mute and ultimate,
the other baffling in its ruffles as a rose.

The largest a valve of bone streaked like a cloud,
its shadowy crease, ambiguous vestibule a puckered trap
ajar.
The sly, inviting smile into the labyrinth.

JAMES WRIGHT

The Minneapolis Poem 102

to John Logan

1.
I wonder how many old men last winter
Hungry and frightened by namelessness prowled
The Mississippi shore
Lashed blind by the wind, dreaming
Of suicide in the river.
The police remove their cadavers by daybreak
And turn them in somewhere.
Where?
How does the city keep lists of its fathers
Who have no names?
By Nicollet Island I gaze down at the dark water
So beautifully slow.
And I wish my brothers good luck
And a warm grave.

2.
The Chippewa young men
Stab one another shrieking
Jesus Christ.
Split-lipped homosexuals limp in terror of assault.
High school backfields search under benches
Near the Post Office. Their faces are the rich
Raw bacon without eyes.
The Walker Art Center crowd stare
At the Guthrie Theater.

3.
Tall Negro girls from Chicago
Listen to light songs.
They know when the supposed patron
Is a plainclothesman.

A cop's palm
Is a roach dangling down the scorched fangs
Of a light bulb.
The soul of a cop's eyes
Is an eternity of Sunday daybreak in the suburbs
Of Juárez, Mexico.

4.
The legless beggars are gone, carried away
By white birds.
The Artificial Limbs Exchange is gutted
And sown with lime.
The whalebone crutches and hand-me-down trusses
Huddle together dreaming in a desolation
Of dry groins.
I think of poor men astonished to waken
Exposed in broad daylight by the blade
Of a strange plough.

5.
All over the walls of comb cells
Automobiles perfumed and blindered
Consent with a mutter of high good humor
To take their two naps a day.
Without sound windows glide back
Into dusk.
The sockets of a thousand blind bee graves tier upon tier
Tower not quite toppling.
There are men in this city who labor dawn after dawn
To sell me my death.

6.
But I could not bear
To allow my poor brother my body to die
In Minneapolis.
The old man Walt Whitman our countryman
Is now in America our country
Dead.
But he was not buried in Minneapolis
At least.
And no more may I be
Please God.

7.
I want to be lifted up
By some great white bird unknown to the police,
And soar for a thousand miles and be carefully hidden
Modest and golden as one last corn grain,
Stored with the secrets of the wheat and the mysterious
lives
Of the unnamed poor.

JAMES SCHUYLER

Salute

Past is past, and if one
remembers what one meant
to do and never did, is
not to have thought to do
enough? Like that gather-
ing of one of each I
planned, to gather one
of each kind of clover,
daisy, paintbrush that
grew in that field
the cabin stood in and
study them one afternoon
before they wilted. Past
is past; I salute
that various field.

For John Clare

Kind of empty in the way it sees everything, the earth gets to its feet and salutes the sky. More of a success at it this time than most others it is. The feeling that the sky might be in the back of someone's mind. Then there is no telling how many there are. They grace everything—bush and tree—to take the roisterer's mind off his caroling—so it's like a smooth switch back. To what was aired in their previous conniption fit. There is so much to be seen everywhere that it's like not getting used to it, only there is so much it never feels new, never any different. You are standing looking at that building and you cannot take it all in, certain details are already hazy and the mind boggles. What will it all be like in five years' time when you try to remember? Will there have been boards in between the grass part and the edge of the street? As long as that couple is stopping to look in that window over there we cannot go. We feel like they have to tell us we can, but they never look our way and they are already gone, gone far into the future—the night of time. If we could look at a photograph of it and say there they are, they never really stopped but there they are. There is so much to be said, and on the surface of it very little gets said.

There ought to be room for more things, for a spreading out, like. Being immersed in the details of rock and field and slope—letting them come to you for once, and then meeting them halfway would be so much easier—if they took an ingenuous pride in being in one's blood. Alas, we perceive them if at all as those things that were meant to be put aside—costumes of the supporting actors or voice trilling at the end of a narrow enclosed street. You can do nothing with them. Not even offer to pay.

It is possible that finally, like coming to the end of a long, barely perceptible rise, there is mutual cohesion and interaction. The whole scene is fixed in your mind, the music all present, as though you could see each note as well as hear it. I say this because there is an uneasiness in things just now. Waiting for something to be over before you are forced to notice it. The pollarded trees scarcely bucking the wind—and yet it's keen, it makes you fall over. Clabbered sky. Seasons that pass with a rush. After all it's their time too—nothing says they aren't to make something of it. As for Jenny Wren, she cares, hopping about on her little twig like she was tryin' to tell us somethin', but that's just it, she couldn't even if she wanted to—dumb bird. But the others —and they in some way must know too—it would never occur to them to want to, even if they could take the first step of the terrible journey toward feeling somebody should act, that ends in utter confusion and hopelessness, east of the sun and west of the moon. So their comment is: "No comment." Meanwhile the whole history of probabilities is coming to life, starting in the upper left-hand corner, like a sail.

ROBERT HAYDEN

Locus 108

(for Ralph)

Here redbuds like momentary trees
        of an illusionist;
here Cherokee rose, acacia, and mimosa;
here magnolias—totemic flowers
        wreathing legends of this place.
Here violent metamorphosis,
        with every blossom turning
deadly and memorial soldiers,
their sabres drawn, charging
        firewood shacks,
apartheid streets. Here wound-red earth
        and blinding cottonfields,
rock hills where sachems counseled,
where scouts gazed stealthily
        upon the glittering death march
of De Soto through Indian wilderness.
        Here mockingbird and
cottonmouth, fury of rivers.
Here swamp and trace and bayou
        where the runagate hid,
the devil with Spanish pistols rode.
        Here spareness, rankness, harsh
brilliances; beauty of what's hardbitten,
knotted, stinted, flourishing
        in despite, on thorny meagerness
thriving, twisting into grace.
        Here symbol houses
where the brutal dream lives out its lengthy
dying. Here the past, adored and
        unforgiven. Here the past—
soulscape, Old Testament battleground
of warring shades whose weapons kill.

SYLVIA PLATH

Last Words 109

I do not want a plain box, I want a sarcophagus
With tigery stripes, and a face on it
Round as the moon, to stare up.
I want to be looking at them when they come
Picking among the dumb minerals, the roots.
I see them already—the pale, star-distance faces.
Now they are nothing, they are not even babies.
I imagine them without fathers or mothers, like the first gods.
They will wonder if I was important.
I should sugar and preserve my days like fruit!
My mirror is clouding over—
A few more breaths, and it will reflect nothing at all.
The flowers and the faces whiten to a sheet.

I do not trust the spirit. It escapes like steam
In dreams, through mouth-hole or eye-hole. I can't stop it.
One day it won't come back. Things aren't like that.
They stay, their little particular lusters
Warmed by much handling. They almost purr.
When the soles of my feet grow cold,
The blue eye of my turquoise will comfort me.
Let me have my copper cooking pots, let my rouge pots
Bloom about me like night flowers, with a good smell.
They will roll me up in bandages, they will store my heart
Under my feet in a neat parcel.
I shall hardly know myself. It will be dark,
And the shine of these small things sweeter than the face of Ishtar.

STANLEY KUNITZ

The Testing-Tree 110

1

On my way home from school
up tribal Providence Hill
past the Academy ballpark
where I could never hope to play
I scuffed in the drainage ditch
among the sodden seethe of leaves
hunting for perfect stones
rolled out of glacial time
into my pitcher's hand;
then sprinted lickety-
split on my magic Keds
from a crouching start,
scarcely touching the ground
with my flying skin
as I poured it on
for the prize of the mastery
over that stretch of road,
with no one no where to deny
when I flung myself down
that on the given course
I was the world's fastest human.

2

Around the bend
that tried to loop me home
dawdling came natural
across a nettled field
riddled with rabbit-life
where the bees sank sugar-wells
in the trunks of the maples
and a stringy old lilac
more than two stories tall

blazing with mildew
        remembered a door in the
                long teeth of the woods.
All of it happened slow:
        brushing the stickseed off,
                wading through jewelweed
strangled by angel's hair,
        spotting the print of the deer
                and the red fox's scats.
Once I owned the key
        to an umbrageous trail
                thickened with mosses
where flickering presences
        gave me right of passage
                as I followed in the steps
of straight-backed Massassoit
        soundlessly heel-and-toe
                practicing my Indian walk.

3
Past the abandoned quarry
        where the pale sun bobbed
                in the sump of the granite,
past copperhead ledge,
        where the ferns gave foothold,
                I walked, deliberate,
on to the clearing,
        with the stones in my pocket
                changing to oracles
and my coiled ear tuned
        to the slightest leaf-stir.
                I had kept my appointment.
There I stood in the shadow,

at fifty measured paces,
of the inexhaustible oak,
tyrant and target,
Jehovah of acorns,
watchtower of the thunders,
that locked King Philip's War
in its annulated core
under the cut of my name.
Father wherever you are
I have only three throws
bless my good right arm.
In the haze of afternoon,
while the air flowed saffron,
I played my game for keeps—
for love, for poetry,
and for eternal life—
after the trials of summer.

4
In the recurring dream
my mother stands
in her bridal gown
under the burning lilac,
with Bernard Shaw and Bertie
Russell kissing her hands;
the house behind her is in ruins;
she is wearing an owl's face
and makes barking noises.
Her minatory finger points.
I pass through the cardboard doorway
askew in the field
and peer down a well
where an albino walrus huffs.

He has the gentlest eyes.
If the dirt keeps sifting in,
staining the water yellow,
why should I be blamed?
Never try to explain.
That single Model A
sputtering up the grade
unfurled a highway behind
where the tanks maneuver,
revolving their turrets.
In a murderous time
the heart breaks and breaks
and lives by breaking.
It is necessary to go
through dark and deeper dark
and not to turn.
I am looking for the trail.
Where is my testing-tree?
Give me back my stones!

The Brother

When morning came
I rose and made tea
and sent off my brother.
In the quiet house
I sat down to wait.

The day knocked on my door
with its sack of wares. The evening
looked in my window
with its inconsolable gray eyes.
On the table the lamp was lit.

My brother came home then,
white dust on his shoes
and a tiny blue flower in his cap,
weary
as if he'd danced a long time
or met a girl in the fields.

When I touched his sleeve
my fingers brought away
a fragrance of mint and grass.

Now my brother wants sleep
and moons foolishly at my bed.
What I want
is to wash his feet
and send him off again, tomorrow,
with a stone in each shoe
and one for each hand
and no bread in his pocket.

RICHMOND LATTIMORE

Report from a Planet 115

Those were countries simple to observe, difficult
to interpret. Young men are sage and bearded;
grandmothers
are pretty; the married care little for marriage, but have

many babies; black and white were never so close and
cordial,
and never hated so much; elder counsellors are brainless
but play good tennis. Their heroes, who are genuine

heroes, are also killers. These people can do anything
difficult, but nothing easy: catch and tame sight
and sound out of space; stroll in it; fly tons of steel

and come down on a handkerchief, yet can not realize a
simple
covenant. Hundreds of wise men are united by subtle
communication, to form one mind and talk like a single
idiot.

We have seen angels dropping fire on straw villages,
and fiends sentimentally entertained by pitiful
musicians imitating the entertainers of angels.

We have seen more good than ever we saw before
accomplishing unendurable evil.

We have seen a whole world ruled by a handful of men.
No two from one country.

CONSTANCE CARRIER

Transformation Scene 116

> *"But there is the danger,"* he said, *"of trying to keep*
> *the past alive at the expense of one's own reality . . ."*

Returned, a wraith from her defrauded tomb,
she haunts an empty house,
stares through a window at a scrawl of boughs,
wanders from room to legendary room.

Weightless, she roams; with printless fingertips
touches the polished table-tops, and looks
at the long rows of books;
turns then, and slips

through an unopened door and past the stair.
Nothing can be neglected; she must check
lest there be change, lest there be flaw or fleck
to dim the house whose keeping is her care . . .

till, in a sunlight grown lackluster, she
who cast no shadow even in full sun,
comes on a mirror where there should be none,
sees her reflection who had none to see—

watches it sharpen, grow opaque and clear,
while silence gathers and like summer thunder
splits the high cupola, swells downward under
a gray light, and explodes upon her ear

here in a house that will not fall but fade
as her own body takes on life once more.
Not she is unsubstantial, but the door
she passes through, its locks again betrayed.

She walks on ground grown firm; the house, receding,
dissolves behind her. From a bough she breaks
a branch of blossom, and the branch-end rakes
her arm, her flesh, warm in the sun, and bleeding.

JOHN BALABAN

The Guard at the Binh Thuy Bridge 118

How still he stands as mists begin to move,
as morning, curling, billows creep across
his cooplike, concrete sentry perched mid-bridge
over mid-muddy river. Stares at bush green banks
which bristle rifles, mortars, men—perhaps.
No convoys shake the timbers. No sound
but water slapping boat sides, bank sides, pilings.
He's slung his carbine barrel down to keep
the boring dry, and two banana-clips instead of one
are taped to make, now, forty rounds instead
of twenty. Droplets bead from stock to sight;
they bulb, then strike his boot. He scrapes his heel,
and sees no box bombs floating towards his bridge.
Anchored in red morning mist a narrow junk
rocks its weight. A woman kneels on deck
staring at lapping water. Wets her face.
Idly the thick Rach Binh Thuy slides by.
He aims. At her. Then drops his aim. Idly.

JOSEPHINE MILES

Family 119

When you swim in the surf off Seal Rocks, and your
family
Sits in the sand
Eating potato salad, and the undertow
Comes which takes you out away down
To loss of breath loss of play and the power of play
Holler, say
Help, help, help. Hello, they will say,
Come back here for some potato salad.

It is then that a seventeen year old cub
Cruising in a helicopter from Antigua,
A jackstraw expert speaking only Swedish
And remote from this area as a camel, says
Look down there, there is somebody drowning.
And it is you. You say, yes, yes,
And he throws you a line.
This is what is called the brotherhood of man.

DANIEL HOFFMAN

The Center of Attention

As grit swirls in the wind the word spreads.
On pavements approaching the bridge a crowd
Springs up like mushrooms.
They are hushed at first, intently

Looking. At the top of the pylon
The target of their gaze leans toward them.
The sky sobs
With the sirens of disaster crews

Careening toward the crowd with nets,
Ladders, resuscitation gear, their First
Aid attendants antiseptic in white duck.
The police, strapped into their holsters,

Exert themselves in crowd-control. They can't
Control the situation.
Atop the pylon there's a man who threatens
Violence. He shouts, *I'm gonna jump*—

And from the river of upturned faces
—Construction workers pausing in their construction
work,
Shoppers diverted from their shopping,
The idlers relishing this diversion

In the vacuity of their day—arises
A chorus of cries—*Jump!*
Jump! and *No*—
Come down! Come down! Maybe, if he can hear them,

They seem to be saying *Jump down!* The truth is,
The crowd cannot make up its mind.

This is a tough decision. The man beside me
Reaches into his lunchbox and lets him have it.

Jump! before he bites his sandwich,
While next to him a young blonde clutches
Her handbag to her breasts and moans
Don't *Don't* *Don't* so very softly

You'd think she was afraid of being heard.
The will of the people is divided.
Up there he hasn't made his mind up either.
He has climbed and climbed on spikes imbedded in the
pylon

To get where he has arrived at.
Is he sure now that this is where he was going?
He looks down one way into the river.
He looks down the other way into the people.

He seems to be looking for something
Or for somebody in particular.
Is there anyone here who is that person
Or can give him what it is that he needs?

From the back of a firetruck a ladder teeters.
Inching along, up up up up up, a policeman
Holds on with one hand, sliding it on ahead of him.
In the other, outstretched, a pack of cigarettes.

Soon the man will decide between
The creature comfort of one more smoke
And surcease from being a creature.
Meanwhile the crowd calls *Jump!* and calls *Come down!*

Now, his cassock billowing in the bulges of Death's black
flag,
A priest creeps up the ladder too
What will the priest and the policeman together
Persuade the man to do?

He has turned his back to them.
He has turned away from everyone.
His solitariness is nearly complete.
He is alone with his decision.

No one on the ground or halfway into the sky can know
The hugeness of the emptiness that surrounds him.
All of his senses are orphans.
His ribs are cold andirons.

Does he regret his rejection of furtive pills,
Of closet noose or engine idling in closed garage?
A body will plummet through shrieking air,
The audience dumb with horror, the spattered street . . .

The world he has left is as small as toys at his feet.
Where he stands, though nearer the sun, the wind is
chill.
He clutches his arms—a caress, or is he trying
Merely to warm himself with his arms?

The people below, their necks are beginning to ache.
They are getting impatient for this diversion
To come to some conclusion. The priest
Inches further narrowly up the ladder.

The center of everybody's attention
For some reason has lit up a butt. He sits down.
He looks down on the people gathered, and sprinkles
Some of his ashes upon them.

Before he is halfway down
The crowd is half-dispersed.
It was his aloneness that clutched them together.
They were spellbound by his despair

And now each rung brings him nearer,
Nearer to their condition
Which is not sufficiently interesting
To detain them from business or idleness either,

Or is too close to a despair
They do not dare
Exhibit before a crowd
Or admit to themselves they share.

Now the police are taking notes
On clipboards, filling the forms.
He looks round as though searching for what he came
    down for.
Traffic flows over the bridge.

RICHARD HUGO

Plans for Altering the River

Those who favor our plan to alter the river
raise your hand. Thank you for your vote.
Last week, you'll recall, I spoke about how water
never complains. How it runs where you tell it,
seemingly at home, flooding grain or pinched
by geometric banks like those in this graphic
depiction of our plan. We ask for power:
a river boils or falls to turn our turbines.
The river approves our plans to alter the river.

Due to a shipwreck downstream, I'm sad to report
our project is not on schedule. The boat
was carrying cement for our concrete rip rap
balustrade that will force the river to run
east of the factory site through the state-owned
grove of cedar. Then, the uncooperative
carpenters union went on strike. When we get
that settled, and the concrete, given good weather
we can go ahead with our plan to alter the river.

We have the injunction. We silenced the opposition.
The workers are back. The materials arrived
and everything's humming. I thank you
for this award, this handsome plaque I'll keep
forever above my mantel, and I'll read
the inscription often aloud to remind me
how with your courageous backing I fought
our battle and won. I'll always remember
this banquet this day we started to alter the river.

Flowers on the bank? A park on Forgotten Island?
Return of cedar and salmon? Who are these men?
These Johnnys-come-lately with plans to alter the river?

What's this wild festival in May
celebrating the runoff, display floats on fire
at night and a forest dance under the stars?
Children sing through my locked door, 'Old stranger,
we're going to alter, to alter, alter the river.'
Just when the water was settled and at home.

Illustrious One, in whom death is the vagrom wound
& who wanders on the wet grasses singing, sing no more
to me. I have heard your voice plenty & I hunger for
health.
Yes, though it is beautiful & seduces, Hush. Come no
more
glaze-eyed to my arms asking for pity then push me aside
when the urge strikes to start singing. Transfixed
& then unhinged, crazed with the wish to die & then
with the fear
the wish might be granted. I have heard your song
and it shall not drag me yet down with it on the wet
grasses.

Illustrious One, in whom death goes on living season by
season,
drawing its strength from your singing, lovely
& deadly, Listen: I will not make myself
dead to nourish the death
blooming within you, vagrom intensity. Rather than that
I'd see
you wandering lost on the white watery lawns at
midnight
singing for the police to come get you, yes, even rather
see you staring at a white wall trying to sing the shapes
out of the whiteness than continue this dying together.

Illustrious One, in whom death is no longer a solid block
but a network, sing no more to me of the waterglass &
the stopped clock.
Against such songs we've crashed enough, enough.
That which was from the heart and was heart's song
has been transformed, a heartless net in which to sing

is to struggle and suffer humiliation at the hour of death.
You who sing out of the vagrom flower-mouth-wound, go
back!
The white grasses will release you, bones & voice & dress
one entity, dignity regained, deathsong left where you
leave
your shape on the lawn in the wet blades. Singing yet.

ELIZABETH BISHOP

Poem 128

About the size of an old-style dollar bill,
American or Canadian,
mostly the same whites, gray greens, and steel grays
—this little painting (a sketch for a larger one?)
has never earned any money in its life.
Useless and free, it has spent seventy years
as a minor family relic
handed along collaterally to owners
who looked at it sometimes, or didn't bother to.

It must be Nova Scotia; only there
does one see gabled wooden houses
painted that awful shade of brown.
The other houses, the bits that show, are white.
Elm trees, low hills, a thin church steeple
—that gray-blue wisp—or is it? In the foreground
a water meadow with some tiny cows,
two brushstrokes each, but confidently cows;
two minuscule white geese in the blue water,
back-to-back, feeding, and a slanting stick.
Up closer, a wild iris, white and yellow,
fresh-squiggled from the tube.
The air is fresh and cold; cold early spring
clear as gray glass; a half inch of blue sky
below the steel-gray storm clouds.
(They were the artist's specialty.)
A specklike bird is flying to the left.
Or is it a flyspeck looking like a bird?

Heavens, I recognize the place, I know it!
It's behind—I can almost remember the farmer's name.
His barn backed on that meadow. There it is,
titanium white, one dab. The hint of steeple,

filaments of brush-hairs, barely there,
must be the Presbyterian church.
Would that be Miss Gillespie's house?
Those particular geese and cows
are naturally before my time.

A sketch done in an hour, "in one breath,"
once taken from a trunk and handed over.
Would you like this? I'll probably never
have room to hang these things again.
Your Uncle George, no, mine, my Uncle George,
he'd be your great-uncle, left them all with Mother
when he went back to England.
You know, he was quite famous, an R.A. . . .

I never knew him. We both knew this place,
apparently, this literal small backwater,
looked at it long enough to memorize it,
our years apart. How strange. And it's still loved,
or its memory is (it must have changed a lot).
Our visions coincided—"visions" is
too serious a word—our looks, two looks:
art "copying from life" and life itself,
life and the memory of it so compressed
they've turned into each other. Which is which?
Life and the memory of it cramped,
dim, on a piece of Bristol board,
dim, but how live, how touching in detail
—the little that we get for free,
the little of our earthly trust. Not much.
About the size of our abidance

along with theirs: the munching cows,
the iris, crisp and shivering, the water
still standing from spring freshets,
the yet-to-be-dismantled elms, the geese.

PHILIP BOOTH

Stove 131

I wake up in the bed my grandmother died in.
November rain. The whole house is cold.
Long stairs, two rooms through to the kitchen:
walls that haven't been painted
in sixty years. They must have shone then:
pale sun, new pumpkin, old pine.

Nothing shines now but the nickel trim
on the grandmother stove, an iron invention
the whole room leans to surround; even
when it is dead the dogs sleep close behind it.
Now they bark out, but let rain return them;
they can smell how the stove is going to be lit.

Small chips of pine from the woodshed. Then
hardwood kindling. I build it all into the firebox,
on top of loose wads of last June's *Bangor News*.
Under the grate, my first match
catches. Flames congregate, the dogs watch,
the stove begins to attend old wisdom.

After the first noisy moments, I listen for Lora;
she cooked all the mornings my grandmother died,
she ruled the whole kitchen the year I was seven:
I can see Boyd Varnum, a post outside the side door;
he's waiting for Lora, up in the front of the house,
to get right change for his winter squash. Lora says

Boyd's got the best winter squash in the village.
When Boyd gets paid, she ties her apron back on
and lets in the eggman. He has a green wagon.
Lora tells him how last night her husband hit her;
she shows him the marks. All her bruised arms

adjust dampers and vents; under the plates where turnips
are coming to boil, she shifts both pies in the oven.
The dogs feel warmer now. I bank on thick coal.
The panes steam up as sure as November: rain,
school, a talkative stove to come home to at noon;
and Lora sets my red mittens to dry on the nickel shelves
next to the stovepipe. Lora knitted my mittens.

I can still smell the litter of spaniels
whelped between the stove and the wall; there's
venison cooking, there's milktoast being warmed on
the furthest back plate, milktoast to send upstairs
to my dead mother's mother. Because, Lora says,
she is sick. Lora says she is awful sick. When Lora goes
up

to my grandmother's bed, I play with the puppies
under the stove; after they suckle and go back to sleep,
because I am in second grade and am seven, I practice
reading the black iron letters raised on the black oven
door;
even though I don't know who Queen Clarion was,
I'm proud I can read what the oven door says: it says

Queen Clarion
Wood & Bishop
Bangor, Maine
1911

It stepped into my room:
A deep, yet luminous shadow clung to the wall,
Steadied itself, then came up taller,
And took on character.
                                        It turned its head,
Smiled, bent over me:
Portly, red-cheeked, benign.
                                                It was Dudley Fitts:
" 'From Carthage I have come—'
All in quotation marks," he said,
"By God, I am a pedant. I always 'pull
For Prime.'
                    Do you hear bells ringing?
When I read aloud
                                Death of Patrokles,
ILIAD, BOOK XVI,
                                I made a schoolboy football-captain
                                    weep!
O Helios-Achilles, thy brightness over me!
And with Meleager of Gadara
                                                I walked with Heliodora:
Petals in her hair: white violets, narcissi,
Myrtle, and chiming lilies,
Innocent crocus, dark, clever hyacinths,
Roses, heavy with dew—
                                        Heliodora, Heliodora."
Behind his voice, there were strains of music:
Vivaldi at Evensong.
                                And above the altar,
Dudley at the keys.
                                Beyond the transept,
Gold shafts of light,
                                then increasing darkness,

And his voice again,
"Being a thimbleful of ashes
Among the shades,
I have enjoyed a loss of earth.
I have come a long way
after Death."

JAMES MERRILL

Lost in Translation

(For Richard Howard)

Diese Tage, die leer dir scheinen
und wertlos für das All,
haben Wurzeln zwischen den Steinen
und trinken dort überall.

A card table in the library stands ready
To receive the puzzle which keeps never coming.
Daylight shines in or lamplight down
Upon the tense oasis of green felt.
Full of unfulfillment, life goes on,
Mirage arisen from time's trickling sands
Or fallen piecemeal into place:
German lesson, picnic, see-saw, walk
With the collie who "did everything but talk"—
Sour windfalls of the orchard back of us.
A summer without parents is the puzzle,
Or should be. But the boy, day after day,
Writes in his Line-a-Day *No puzzle.*

He's in love, at least. His French Mademoiselle,
In real life a widow since Verdun,
Is stout, plain, carrot-haired, devout.
She prays for him, as does a curé in Alsace,
Sews costumes for his marionettes,
Helps him to keep behind the scene
Whose sidelit goosegirl, speaking with his voice,
Plays Guinevere as well as Gunmoll Jean.
Or else at bedtime in his tight embrace
Tells him her own French hopes, her German fears,
Her—but what more is there to tell?
Having known grief and hardship, Mademoiselle
Knows little more. Her languages. Her place.

Noon coffee. Mail. The watch that also waited
Pinned to her heart, poor gold, throws up its hands—
No puzzle! Steaming bitterness
Her sugars draw pops back into his mouth, translated:
"Patience, chéri. Geduld, mein Schatz."
(Thus, reading Valéry the other evening
And seeming to recall a Rilke version of "Palme,"
That sunlit paradigm whereby the tree
Taps a sweet wellspring of authority,
The hour came back. Patience dans l'azur.
Geduld im . . . Himmelblau? Mademoiselle.)

Out of the blue, as promised, of a New York
Puzzle-rental shop the puzzle comes—
A superior one, containing a thousand hand-sawn,
Sandal-scented pieces. Many take
Shapes known already—the craftsman's repertoire
Nice in its limitation—from other puzzles:
Witch on broomstick, ostrich, hourglass,
Even (surely not just in retrospect)
An inchling, innocently branching palm.
These can be put aside, made stories of
While Mademoiselle spreads out the rest face-up,
Herself excited as a child; or questioned
Like incoherent faces in a crowd,
Each with its scrap of highly colored
Evidence the Law must piece together.
Sky-blue ostrich? Likely story.
Mauve of the witch's cloak white, severed fingers
Pluck? Detain her. The plot thickens
As all at once two pieces interlock.

Mademoiselle does borders—(Not so fast.
A London dusk, December last.
Chatter silenced in the library
This grown man reenters, wearing gray.
A medium. All except him have seen
Panel slid back, recess explored,
An object at once unique and common
Displayed, planted in a plain tole
Casket the subject now considers
Through shut eyes, saying in effect:
"Even as voices reach me vaguely
A dry saw-shriek drowns them out,
Some loud machinery—a lumber mill?
Far uphill in the fir forest
Trees tower, tense with shock,
Groaning and cracking as they crash groundward.
But hidden here is a freak fragment
Of a pattern complex in appearance only.
What it seems to show is superficial
Next to that long-term lamination
Of hazard and craft, the karma that has
Made it matter in the first place.
Plywood. Piece of a puzzle." Applause
Acknowledged by an opening of lids
Upon the thing itself. A sudden dread—
But to go back. All this lay years ahead.)

Mademoiselle does borders. Straight-edge pieces
Align themselves with earth or sky
In twos and threes, naive cosmogonists
Whose views clash. Nomad inlanders meanwhile
Begin to cluster where the totem
Of a certain vibrant egg-yolk yellow

Or pelt of what emerging animal
Acts on the straggler like a trumpet call
To form a more sophisticated unit.
By suppertime two ragged wooden clouds
Have formed. In one, a Sheik with beard
And flashing sword hilt (he is all but finished)
Steps forward on a tiger skin. A piece
Snaps shut, and fangs gnash out at us!
In the second cloud—they gaze from cloud to cloud
With marked if undecipherable feeling—
Most of a dark-eyed woman veiled in mauve
Is being helped down from her camel (kneeling)
By a small backward-looking slave or page-boy
(Her son, thinks Mademoiselle mistakenly)
Whose feet have not been found. But lucky finds
In the last minutes before bed
Anchor both factions to the scene's limits
And, by so doing, orient
Them eye to eye across the green abyss.
The yellow promises, oh bliss,
To be in time a sumptuous tent.

Puzzle begun I write in the day's space
Then, while she bathes, peek at Mademoiselle's
Page to the curé: ". . . cette innocente mère,
Ce pauvre enfant, que deviendront-ils?"
Her azure script is curlicued like pieces
Of the puzzle she will be telling him about.
(Fearful incuriosity of childhood!
"Tu as l'accent allemand," said Dominique.
Indeed. Mademoiselle was only French by marriage.
Child of an English mother, a remote
Descendant of the great explorer Speke,

And Prussian father. No one knew. I heard it
Long afterwards from her nephew, a UN
Interpreter. His matter-of-fact account
Touched old strings. My poor Mademoiselle,
With 1939 about to shake
This world where "each was the enemy, each the friend"
To its foundations, kept, though signed in blood,
Her peace a shameful secret to the end.)
"Schlaf wohl, chéri." Her kiss. Her thumb
Crossing my brow against the dreams to come.

This World that shifts like sand, its unforeseen
Consolidations and elate routine,
Whose Potentate had lacked a retinue?
Lo! it assembles on the shrinking Green.

Gunmetal-skinned or pale, all plumes and scars,
Of Vassalage the noblest avatars—
The very coffee-bearer in his vair
Vest is a swart Highness, next to ours.

Kef easing Boredom, and iced syrups, thirst,
In guessed-at glooms old wives who know the worst
Outsweat that virile fiction of the New:
"Insh'Allah, he will tire—" "—or kill her first!"

(Hardly a proper subject for the Home,
Work of—dear Richard, I shall let *you* comb
Archives and learned journals for his name—
A minor lion attending on Gérôme.)

While, thick as Thebes whose presently complete
Gates close behind them, Houri and Afreet

Both claim the Page. He wonders whom to serve,
And what his duties are, and where his feet,
And if we'll find, as some before us did,
That piece of Distance deep in which lies hid
Your tiny apex sugary with sun,
Eternal Triangle, Great Pyramid!

Then sky alone is left, a hundred blue
Fragments in revolution, with no clue
To where a Niche will open. Quite a task,
Putting together Heaven, yet we do.

It's done. Here under the table all along
Were those missing feet. It's done.
The dog's tail thumping. Mademoiselle sketching
Costumes for a coming harem drama
To star the goosegirl. All too soon the swift
Dismantling. Lifted by two corners,
The puzzle hung together—and did not.
Irresistibly a populace,
Unstitched of its attachments, rattled down.
Power went to pieces as the witch
Slithered easily from Virtue's gown.
The blue held out for time, but crumbled, too.
The city had long fallen, and the tent,
A separating sauce mousseline,
Been swept away. Remained the green
On which the grown-ups gambled. A green dusk.
First lightning bugs. Last glow of west
Green in the false eyes of (coincidence)
Our mangy tiger safe on his bared hearth.

Before the puzzle was boxed and readdressed
To the puzzle shop in the mid-Sixties,
Something tells me that one piece contrived
To stay in the boy's pocket. How do I know?
I know because so many later puzzles
Had missing pieces—Maggie Teyte's high notes
Gone at the war's end, end of the vogue for collies,
A house torn down; and hadn't Mademoiselle
Kept back her pitiful bit of truth as well?
I've spent the last days, furthermore,
Ransacking Athens for that translation of "Palme."
Neither the Goethehaus nor the National Library
Seems able to unearth it. Yet I can't
Just be imagining. I've seen it. Know
How much of the sun-ripe original
Felicity Rilke made himself forego
(Who loved French words—verger, mûr, parfumer)
In order to render its underlying sense.
Know already in that tongue of his
What Pains, what monolithic Truths
Shadow stanza to stanza's symmetrical
Rhyme-rutted pavement. Know that ground plan left
Sublime and barren, where the warm Romance
Stone by stone faded, cooled; the fluted nouns
Made taller, lonelier than life
By leaf-carved capitals in the afterglow.
The owlet umlaut peeps and hoots
Above the open vowel. And after rain
A deep reverberation fills with stars.

Lost, is it, buried? One more missing piece?

But nothing's lost. Or else: all is translation
And every bit of us is lost in it
(Or found—I wander through the ruin of S
Now and then, wondering at the peacefulness)
And in that loss a self-effacing tree,
Color of context, imperceptibly
Rustling with its angel, turns the waste
To shade and fiber, milk and memory.

JANE COOPER

Rent

If you want my apartment, sleep in it
but let's have a clear understanding:
the books are still free agents.

If the rocking chair's arms surround you
they can also let you go,
they can shape the air like a body.

I don't want your rent, I want
a radiance of attention
like the candle's flame when we eat,

I mean a kind of awe
attending the spaces between us—
Not a roof but a field of stars.

LAURA GILPIN

The Two-Headed Calf

Tomorrow when the farm boys find this
freak of nature, they will wrap his body
in newspaper and carry him to the museum.

But tonight he is alive and in the north
field with his mother. It is a perfect
summer evening: the moon rising over
the orchard, the wind in the grass. And
as he stares into the sky, there are
twice as many stars as usual.

ROBERT MEZEY

Couplets, XX

Don't be afraid of dying. The glass of water
Is quickly poured into the waiting goblet.

Your face that will be of no further use to mirrors
Grows more and more transparent, nothing is hidden.

It's night in the remotest provinces of the brain,
Seeing falls back into the great sea of light.

How strange to see that glittering green fly
Walk onto the eyeball, rubbing its hands and praying.

Don't be afraid, you're going to where you were
Before birth pushed you into this cold light.

Lie down here, next to Empedocles;
Be joined to the small grains of the brotherhood.

EDWARD FIELD

Mae West

She comes on drenched in a perfume called Self
    Satisfaction
from feather boa to silver pumps.

She does not need to be loved by you
though she'll give you credit for good taste.
Just because you say you love her
she's not throwing herself at your feet in gratitude.

Every other star reveals how worthless she feels
by crying when the hero says he loves her,
or how unhoped-for the approval is
when the audience applauds her big number—
but Mae West takes it as her due.
She knows she's good.

She expects the best for herself
and knows she's worth what she costs,
and she costs plenty.
She's not giving anything away.

She enjoys her admirers, fat daddy or muscleman,
and doesn't confuse vanity and sex,
though she never turns down pleasure,
lapping it up.

Above all she enjoys her Self,
swinging her body that says, Me me me me.
Why not have a good time?
As long as you amuse me, go on,
I like you slobbering over my hand, big boy.
I have a right to.

Most convincing, we know all this
not by her preaching it
but by her presence—it's no act.
Every word and look and movement
spells independence:
She likes being herself.

And we who don't
can only look on, astonished.

DONALD HALL

Ox Cart Man 148

In October of the year,
he counts potatoes dug from the brown field,
counting the seed, counting
the cellar's portion out,
and bags the rest on the cart's floor.

He packs wool sheared in April, honey
in combs, linen, leather
tanned from deerhide,
and vinegar in a barrel
hooped by hand at the forge's fire.

He walks by his ox's head, ten days
to Portsmouth Market, and sells potatoes,
and the bag that carried potatoes,
flaxseed, birch brooms, maple sugar, goose
feathers, yarn.

When the cart is empty he sells the cart.
When the cart is sold he sells the ox,
harness and yoke, and walks
home, his pockets heavy
with the year's coin for salt and taxes,

and at home by fire's light in November cold
stitches new harness
for next year's ox in the barn,
and carves the yoke, and saws planks
building the cart again.

At the song's beginning
Even as our voices
Rise we know the last words

And what it will sound like
To sing them at the end
Of the final burden;

Just so the cold fiddler
Hums the final chords of
Each of our capriccios

Even as he starts up.
But Jack, looking out of
The house that our song had

Him build, can see no cock
Crowing in the morn at
Break of ultimate day:

How then can we now shape
Our last stanza, furnish
This chamber of codas?

Here in the pale tan of
The yet ungathered grain
There may be time to chant

The epic of whispers
In the light of a last
Candle that may be made

To outlast its waning
Wax, a frail flame shaking
In a simulacrum

Of respiration. Oh,
We shall carry it set
Down inside a pitcher

Out into the field, late
Wonderers errant in
Among the rich flowers.

Like a star reflected
In a cup of water,
It will light up no path:

Neither will it go out.
Here at the easternmost
Edge of the sunset world

Starlings perch like quick notes
On a stave of wires high
Against the page of sky

But silently: in a
Mown oatfield what text will
The dallying night leave?

—A tree of light. A bush
Unconsumed by its fire.
Branches of flame given

Sevenfold tongue that there
Might be recompounded
Out of the smashed vessels

Of oil, of blood and stain,
Wine of grass and juice of
Violet, a final

White, here at the point of
Sky water and field all
Plunged in their own deep well

Of color whose bottom
Is all of the darkness.
If clear water is to

Give light, let it be here.
And if sound beyond breath
Of candle flame endure,

Then no wailful choir of
Natural small songs, no
Blend of winds; but let be

Heard their one undersong
Filling this vast chamber
Of continuing air

With the flickering of
Cantillation, quickened
Soon in the ringing dew.

Now, at the eastern edge of the black grass, he drinks a draught of the juice of the last flower.

Ten black drops have been flung into the night, as if by his little finger dipped into the deepest of cups;

And he considers the three higher colors that have been beyond color always; and he considers these at the dying of the wise light, remembering childhood:

In the chemist's window it was the same water that bubbled up through the differently colored glass tubes, even as oil streams forth into the lights, all the lights.

In the chemist's window, the hanging spheres of ruby, of emerald, of amber: he was told "Those are colored water" not as if a radiance had been selectively stained, but as if the colorless had been awakened from its long exile in mere transparency.

The diaspora of water ends when those colored bowls give back nothing that is untimed by their own light.

The eternities of the book end when there is only light for one eye, when the chant can be heard by only one ear: the hidden candle, the locked clavichord of implications.

Here they all were: The unfolding of What There Was
The warring of the leaves
The shaping of the rounded spore
And all that occurred therein
The opening of the codex

The echoes of wars, the shades of
    shaping
And the shadows of the echoes of
    the told told tales

They all end by the black grass, where fireflies dart about busily flickering with their hopeless fictions,

And the fiction that the first text was itself a recension of whispers, a gathering of what had been half-heard among the trees.

When morning comes, they will stop and go out, though morning will bring no light along the right-hand path on the margin of the dark.

It will be only his old man's dream of dawn that unrobes the violet, allows the early rose to take her morning dip.

He remembers this, and thinks not to quest among the regions of black for what lies beyond violet,

But would stay to hum his hymn of the hedges, where truth is one letter away from death, and will ever so be emended.

Blessed be who has crushed the olive for the oil.

Blessed be who has cracked the oil for the light.

Blessed be who has buried the light for the three tones beyond,

In which, when we have been stamped out and burned not to lie in the ashes of our dust, it will be to grow.

I.

Beyond the last house, where home was,
Past the marsh we found the old skull in, all nameless
And cracked in a star-shape from stone-smack,
Up the hill where the grass was tangled waist-high and
wind-tousled,
To the single great oak that, in leaf-season, hung like
A thunderhead black against whatever blue the sky had,

And here, at the widest circumference of shade, when
shade was,
Ran the trench, six feet long,
And wide enough for a man to lie down in,
In comfort, if comfort was still any object. No sign there
Of any ruined cabin, foundation, or well,
So Pap must have died of camp-fever,
And the others pushed on, God knows where.

II.

The Dark and Bloody Ground, so the teacher
romantically said,
But one look out the window, and woods and ruined
cornfields we saw:
A careless flung corner of country, no hope and no
history here.
No hope but the Pullman lights that swept
Night-fields—glass-glint from some farmhouse and flicker
of ditches—
Or the night freight's moan on the rise where
You might catch a ride on the rods,
Just for hell, or if need had arisen.
No history either—no Harrod, or Finley, or Boone.

No tale how the Bluebellies broke at the Rebel yell and
  cold steel.

So we had to invent it all, our Bloody Ground, K and I,
And him the best shot in ten counties and could call any
  bird-note back,
But school out, not big enough for the ballgame,
And in the full tide of summer, not ready
For the twelve-gauge yet, or even a job, so what
Can you do but pick up your BBs and Benjamin,
Stick corn pone in pocket, and head out
"To Rally in the Cane-Brake and Shoot the Buffalo"—
As my grandfather's cracked old voice would sing it
From days of his own grandfather—and often enough
It was only a Plymouth Rock, or maybe a fat
  Dominecker,
That fell to the crack of the unerring Decherd.

III.

Yes, imagination is strong. But not strong enough in the
  face of
The sticky feathers and BBs a mother's hand held out.
But no liberal concern was evinced for the Redskin,
As we trailed and out-tricked the sly Shawnees
In a thicket of ironweed, and I wrestled one naked
And slick with his bear-grease, till my hunting knife
Bit home, and the tomahawk
Slipped from his hand. And what mother cared about
  Bluebellies,
Who came charging our trench? But we held
To pour the last volley at face-gape before
The tangle and clangor of bayonet.

Yes, a day is merely forever
In memory's shiningness,
And a year but a gust or a gasp
In the summer's heat of Time, and in that last summer
I was almost ready to learn
What imagination is—it is only
The lie we must learn to live by, if ever
We mean to live at all. Times change.
Things change. And K up and gone, and the summer
Gone, and I yearned to know the world's name.

IV.

Well, what I remember most
In a world, long Time-paled and powdered
Like a vision still clinging to plaster
Set by Piero della Francesca,
Is how K, through lane-dust or meadow,
Seemed never to walk, but float
With a singular joy and silence,
In his cloud of bird dogs, like angels
With their eyes on his eyes like God,
And the sun on his uncut hair bright
As he passed through the ramshackle town and
odd folks there
With pants on and vests and always soft gabble of
money—
Polite in his smiling, but never much to say.

V.

To pass through to what? No, not
To some wild white peak dreamed westward,
And each sunrise a promise to keep. No, only

The Big Leagues, not even a bird dog,
And girls that popped gum while they screwed.

Yes, that was his path, and no batter
Could do what booze finally did:
Just blow him off the mound—but anyway,
He had always called it a fool game, just something
For children who hadn't yet dreamed what
A man is, or barked a squirrel, or raised
A single dog from a pup.

VI.

And I, too, went on my way, the winning or losing, or
what
Is sometimes of all things the worst, the not knowing
One thing from the other, nor knowing
How the teeth in Time's jaws all snag backward,
And whatever enters therein
Has less hope of remission than shark-meat,

And one Sunday afternoon, in the idleness of summer,
I found his farm and him home there,
With the bird dogs crouched round in the grass,
And their eyes on his eyes as he whispered
Whatever to bird dogs it was.
Then yelled: "Well, for Christ's sake, it's you!"

Yes, me, for Christ's sake, and some sixty
Years blown like a hurricane past! But what can you say—
Can you say—when *all-to-be-said* is the *done*?
So our talk ran to buffalo hunting, and the look on his
mother's face,

And the sun sank low as he stood there,
All Indian-brown from waist up, who never liked tops to
his pants,
And standing nigh straight, but the arms and the pitcher's
Great shoulders, they were thinning to old-man thin.
Sun low, all silence, then sudden:
"But Jesus," he cried, "what makes a man do what he
does—
Him living until he dies!"

Sure all of us live till we die, but bingo!
Like young David at brookside, he swooped down,
Snatched a stone, wound up, and let fly,
And high on a pole over yonder the big brown insulator
Simply exploded. "See, I still got control!" he said.

VII.

Late, late, toward sunset, I wandered
Where old dreams had once been Life's truth, and where
Sank the trench of our valor, now nothing
But a ditch full of late-season weed-growth,
Beyond the rim of shade.

There was nobody there, hence no shame to be saved
from, so I
Just lie in the trench on my back and see high,
Beyond tall ironweed stalks, or oak leaves
If I happened to look that way,
How the late summer's thinned-out sky moves,
Drifting on, drifting on, like forever,
From *where* on to *where,* and I wonder
What it would be like to die,
Like the nameless old skull in the swamp, lost,

And know yourself dead lying under
The infinite motion of sky.

VIII.

But why should I lie here longer?
I am not yet dead though in years,
And the world's way is yet long to go,
And I love the world even in my anger,
And love is a hard thing to outgrow.

breaks up in obelisks on the river,
as I stand beside your grave.
I tip my head back.
Above me, the same sky you loved,
that shawl of cotton wool,
frozen around the shoulders of Minnesota.
I'm cold and so far from Texas
and my father, who gave me to you.
I was twelve, a Choctaw, a burden.
A woman, my father said, raising my skirt.
Then he showed you the roll of green gingham,
stained red, that I'd tried to crush to powder
with my small hands. I close my eyes,

and it is March 1866 again.
I'm fourteen, wearing a white smock.
I straddle the rocking horse you made for me
and stroke the black mane cut from my own hair.
Sunrise hugs you from behind,
as you walk through the open door
and lay the velvet beside me.

I give you the ebony box
with the baby's skull inside
and you set it on your work table,
comb your pale blond hair with one hand,
then nail it shut.
When the new baby starts crying, I cover my ears,

watching as you lift him from the cradle
and lay him on the pony-skin rug.
I untie the red scarf, knotted at my throat,
climb off the horse and bend over you.

I slip the scarf around your neck,
and pull it tight, remembering:
I strangled the other baby,
laid her on your stomach while you were asleep.
You break my hold and pull me to the floor.
I scratch you, bite your lips, your face,
then you cry out,
and I open and close my hands
around a row of bear teeth.

I open my eyes.
I wanted you then and now,
and I never let you know.
I kiss the headstone.
Tonight, wake me like always.
Talk and I'll listen,
while you lie on the pallet
resting your arms behind your head,
telling me about the wild rice in the marshes
and the empty .45 you call *Grace of God* that keeps you
alive,
as we slide forward, without bitterness, decade by decade,
becoming transparent. Everlasting.

Like battered old millhands, they stand in the orchard—
Like drunk legionnaires, heaving themselves up,
Lurching to attention. Not one of them wobbles
The same way as another. Uniforms won't fit them—
All those cramps, humps, bulges. Here, a limb's gone;
There, rain and corruption have eaten the whole core.
They've all grown too tall, too thick, or too something.
Like men bent too long over desks, engines, benches,
Or bent under mailsacks, under loss.
They've seen too much history and bad weather, grown
Around rocks, into high winds, diseases, grown
Too long to be wilful, too long to be changed.

Oh, I could replant, bulldoze the lot,
Get nursery stock, all the latest ornamentals,
Make the whole place look like a suburb,
Each limb sleek as a teenybopper's—pink
To the very crotch—each trunk smoothed, ideal
As the fantasy life of an adman.
We might just own the Arboreal Muscle Beach:
Each tree disguised as its neighbor. Or each disguised
As if not its neighbor—each doing its own thing
Like executives' children.

At least I could prune.
At least I should trim the dead wood; fill holes
Where rain collects and decay starts. Well, I should;
I should. There's a red squirrel nests here someplace.
I live in the hope of hearing one saw-whet owl.
Then, too, they're right about Spring. Bees hum
Through these branches like lascivious intentions. The
white

Petals drift down, sift across the ground; this air's so rich
No man should come here except on a working pass;
No man should leave here without going to confession.
All Fall, apples nearly crack the boughs;
They hang here red as candles in the
White oncoming snow.

Tonight we'll drive down to the bad part of town
To the New Hungarian Bar or the Klub Polski,
To the Old Hellas where we'll eat the new spring lamb;
Drink good *mavrodaphne,* say, at the Laikon Bar,
Send drinks to the dancers, those meatcutters and
    laborers
Who move in their native dances, the archaic forms.
Maybe we'll still find our old crone selling chestnuts,
Whose toothless gums can spit out fifteen languages,
Who turns, there, late at night, in the center of the floor,
Her ancient dry hips wheeling their slow, slow *tsamikos;*
We'll stomp under the tables, whistle, we'll all hiss
Till even the belly dancer leaves, disgraced.

We'll drive back, lushed and vacant, in the first dawn;
Out of the light gray mists may rise our flowering
Orchard, the rough trunks holding their formations
Like elders of Colonus, the old men of Thebes
Tossing their white hair, almost whispering,

Soon, each one of us will be taken
By dark powers under this ground
That drove us here, that warped us.
Not one of us got it his own way.

GALWAY KINNELL

Saint Francis and the Sow

The bud
stands for all things,
even for those things that don't flower,
for everything flowers, from within, of self-blessing;
though sometimes it is necessary
to reteach a thing its loveliness,
to put a hand on its brow
of the flower
and retell it in words and in touch
it is lovely
until it flowers again from within, of self-blessing;
as Saint Francis
put his hand on the creased forehead
of the sow, and told her in words and in touch
blessings of earth on the sow, and the sow
began remembering all down her thick length,
from the earthen snout all the way
through the fodder and slops to the spiritual curl of the tail,
from the hard spininess spiked out from the spine
down through the great broken heart
to the sheer blue milken dreaminess spurting and shuddering
from the fourteen teats into the fourteen mouths sucking and blowing beneath them:
the long, perfect loveliness of sow.

Of them all—those laboring men who knew my first
name
And called out to me as I watched them coming up the
walk;
The ones with birthmarks and missing fingers and red
hair,
Who had worked for my grandfather, and now my
father;
Who had gone home to wash up and put on a clean
shirt;
Who came to the back door Friday evenings for their
checks;
Who drove a Ford coupe and had a second wife and
three kids
And were headed for town to have a drink and buy
groceries—

Of the ones too old to work—in their black shoes laced
up
With hooks, and their string ties, who stood on the
sidewalk
When we were building something, and asked my father
If he remembered the house-moving business back during
The Depression: how you squirmed through all that dust
And broken glass in the crawl space, nudging ten-by-
twelves
Twenty feet long, and lugged the house-jacks behind you
One at a time, setting them up just right. How you
moved
On your back like a crab through darkness, cobwebs
Brushing your face, an iron bar in your hands, a voice
Calling somewhere from outside, asking for a quarter-
turn—

Of them all—plumbers, tinners, roofers, well-diggers,
Carpenters, cement finishers with their padded knees—
I liked the sign-painters best: liked being taken there
By my father, following after him, running my fingers
Along the pipe railing, taking his hand as we climbed up
The concrete embankment to their back-street shop
    looking
Out across the Nickel Plate yard—
                                        liked being left to wander
Among piles of fresh pine planks, tables caked and
    smeared
And stacked with hundreds of bottles and jars leaking
    color
And fragrance, coffee cans jammed with dried brushes,
    skylight
Peppered with dead flies, narrow paths that wound
    among
Signs shrouded with tape and newspaper—all the way
    back
To the airshaft, the blackened sink, the two-burner
    hotplate,
Spoons sticking from china mugs, behind the curtain the
    bed
With its torn army blanket—liked feeling beneath my
    toes
The wood floors patterned with forgotten colors, soft
To the step, darkened with grime and soot from the
    trains—

Liked them most of all—those solemn old men with skin
Bleached and faded as their hair, white muslin caps
Speckled with paint, knuckles and fingers faintly dotted—
Liked them for their listening to him about the sign

He wanted painted, for pretending not to notice me
watching—
For the wooden rod with its black knob resting lightly
Against the primed surface, for the slow sweep and
whisper
Of the brush—liked seeing the ghost letters in pencil
Gradually filling out, fresh and wet and gleaming, words
Forming out of all that darkness, that huge disorder.

A great cry went up from the stockyards and
slaughterhouses, and Death, tired of complaint
and constant abuse, withdrew to his underground garage.
He was still young and his work was a torment.
All over, their power cut, people stalled like street cars.
Their gravity taken away, they began to float.
Without buoyancy, they began to sink. Each person
became a single darkened room. The small hand
pressed firmly against the small of their backs
was suddenly gone and people swirled to a halt
like petals fallen from a flower. Why hurry?
Why get out of bed? People got off subways,
on subways, off subways all at the same stop.
Everywhere clocks languished in antique shops
as their hands composed themselves in sleep.
Without time and decay, people grew less beautiful.
They stopped eating and began to study their feet.
They stopped sleeping and spent weeks following stray
    dogs.
The first to react were remnants of the church.
They falsified miracles: displayed priests posing
as corpses until finally they sneezed or grew lonely.
Then governments called special elections to choose
    those
to join the ranks of the volunteer dead: unhappy people
forced to sit in straight chairs for weeks at a time.
Interest soon dwindled. Then the army seized power
and soldiers ran through the street dabbling the living
with red paint. You're dead, they said. Maybe
tomorrow, people answered, today we're just breathing:
look at the sky, look at the color of the grass.
For without Death each color had grown brighter.
At last a committee of businessmen met together,

because with Death gone money had no value.
They went to where Death was waiting in a white room,
and he sat on the floor and looked like a small boy
with pale blond hair and eyes the color of clear water.
In his lap was a red ball heavy with the absence of life.
The businessmen flattered him. We will make you king,
they said. I am king already, Death answered. We will
print your likeness on all the money of the world.
It is there already, Death answered. We adore you
and will not live without you, the businessmen said.
Death said, I will consider your offer.

How Death was restored to his people:

At first the smallest creatures began to die—
bacteria and certain insects. No one noticed. Then fish
began to float to the surface; lizards and tree toads
toppled from sun-warmed rocks. Still no one saw them.
Then birds began tumbling out of the air,
and as sunlight flickered on the blue feathers
of the jay, brown of the hawk, white of the dove,
then people lifted their heads and pointed to the sky
and from the thirsty streets cries of welcome rose up
like a net to catch the delicate and plummeting bodies.

ANTHONY HECHT

The Transparent Man

I'm mighty glad to see you, Mrs. Curtis,
And thank you very kindly for this visit—
Especially now when all the others here
Are having holiday visitors, and I feel
A little conspicuous and in the way.
It's mainly because of Thanksgiving. All these mothers
And wives and husbands gaze at me soulfully
And feel they should break up their box of chocolates
For a donation, or hand me a chunk of fruitcake.
What they don't understand and never guess
Is that it's better for me without a family;
It's a great blessing. Though I mean no harm.
And as for visitors, why, I have you,
All cheerful, brisk and punctual every Sunday,
Like church, even if the aisles smell of phenol.
And you always bring even better gifts than any
On your book-trolley. Though they mean only good,
Families can become a sort of burden.
I've only got my father, and he won't come,
Poor man, because it would be too much for him.
And for me, too, so it's best the way it is.
He knows, you see, that I will predecease him,
Which is hard enough. It would take a callous man
To come and stand around and watch me failing.
(Now don't you fuss; we both know the plain facts.)
But for him it's even harder. He loved my mother.
They say she looked like me; I suppose she may have.
Or rather, as I grew older I came to look
More and more like she must one time have looked,
And so the prospect for my father now
Of losing me is like having to lose her twice.
I know he frets about me. Dr. Frazer
Tells me he phones in every single day,

Hoping that things will take a turn for the better.
But with leukemia things don't improve.
It's like a sort of blizzard in the bloodstream,
A deep, severe, unseasonable winter,
Burying everything. The white blood cells
Multiply crazily and storm around,
Out of control. The chemotherapy
Hasn't helped much, and it makes my hair fall out.
I know I look a sight, but I don't care.
I care about fewer things; I'm more selective.
It's got so I can't even bring myself
To read through any of your books these days.
It's partly weariness, and partly the fact
That I seem not to care much about the endings,
How things work out, or whether they even do.
What I do instead is sit here by this window
And look out at the trees across the way.
You wouldn't think that was much, but let me tell you,
It keeps me quite intent and occupied.
Now all the leaves are down, you can see the spare,
Delicate structures of the sycamores,
The fine articulation of the beeches.
I have sat here for days studying them,
And I have only just begun to see
What it is that they resemble. One by one,
They stand there like magnificent enlargements
Of the vascular system of the human brain.
I see them there like huge discarnate minds,
Lost in their meditative silences.
The trunks, branches and twigs compose the vessels
That feed and nourish vast immortal thoughts.
So I've assigned them names. There, near the path,
Is the great brain of Beethoven, and Kepler

Haunts the wide spaces of that mountain ash.
This view, you see, has become my Hall of Fame.
It came to me one day when I remembered
Mary Beth Finley who used to play with me
When we were girls. One year her parents gave her
A birthday toy called "The Transparent Man."
It was made of plastic, with different colored organs,
And the circulatory system all mapped out
In rivers of red and blue. She'd ask me over
And the two of us would sit and study him
Together, and do a powerful lot of giggling.
I figure he's most likely the only man
Either of us would ever get to know
Intimately, because Mary Beth became
A Sister of Mercy when she was old enough.
She must be thirty-one; she was a year
Older than I, and about four inches taller.
I used to envy both those advantages
Back in those days. Anyway, I was struck
Right from the start by the sea-weed intricacy,
The fine-haired, silken-threaded filiations
That wove, like Belgian lace, throughout the head.
But this last week it seems I have found myself
Looking beyond, or through, individual trees
At the dense, clustered woodland just behind them,
Where those great, nameless crowds patiently stand.
It's become a sort of complex, ultimate puzzle
And keeps me fascinated. My eyes are twenty-twenty,
Or used to be, but of course I can't unravel
The tousled snarl of intersecting limbs,
That mackled, cinder grayness. It's a riddle
Beyond the eye's solution. Impenetrable.
If there is order in all that anarchy

Of granite mezzotint, that wilderness,
It takes a better eye than mine to see it.
It set me on to wondering how to deal
With such a thickness of particulars,
Deal with it faithfully, you understand,
Without blurring the issue. Of course I know
That within a month the sleeving snows will come
With cold, selective emphases, with massings
And arbitrary contrasts, rendering things
Deceptively simple, thickening the twigs
To frosty veins, bestowing epaulets
And decorations on every birch and aspen.
And the eye, self-satisfied, will be misled,
Thinking the puzzle solved, supposing at last
It can look forth and comprehend the world.
That's when you have to really watch yourself.
So I hope that you won't think me plain ungrateful
For not selecting one of your fine books,
And I take it very kindly that you came
And sat here and let me rattle on this way.

Who can remember back to the first poets,
The greatest ones, greater even than Orpheus?
No one has remembered that far back
Or now considers, among the artifacts
And bones and cantilevered inference
The past is made of, those first and greatest poets,
So lofty and disdainful of renown
They left us not a name to know them by.

They were the ones that in whatever tongue
Worded the world, that were the first to say
Star, water, stone, that said the visible
And made it bring invisibles to view
In wind and time and change, and in the mind
Itself that minded the hitherto idiot world
And spoke the speechless world and sang the towers
Of the city into the astonished sky.

They were the first great listeners, attuned
To interval, relationship, and scale,
The first to say above, beneath, beyond,
Conjurors with love, death, sleep, with bread and wine,
Who having uttered vanished from the world
Leaving no memory but the marvelous
Magical elements, the breathing shapes
And stops of breath we build our Babels of.

MARILYN HACKER

La Fontaine de Vaucluse 176

for Marie Ponsot

"Why write unless you praise the sacred places . . . ?"
Richard Howard: "Audiences"

1

Azure striation swirls beyond the stones
flung in by French papas and German boys.
The radio-guide emits trilingual noise.
"Always 'two ladies alone'; we were not alone."
Source, cunt, umbilicus, resilient blue
springs where the sheer gorge spreads wooded, mossed thighs:
unsounded female depth in a child-sized
pool boys throw rocks at. Hobbled in platform shoes,
girls stare from the edge. We came for the day
on a hot bus from Avignon. A Swed-
ish child hurls a chalk boulder; a tall girl,
his sister, twelve, tanned, crouches to finger shell-
whorls bedded in rock-moss. We find our way
here when we can; we take away what we need.

2

Here, when we can, we take away what we need:
stones, jars of herb-leaves, scrap-patch workbags stored
in the haphazard rooms we can afford.
Marie and I are lucky: we can feed
our children and ourselves on what we earn.
One left the man who beat her, left hostages
two daughters; one weighs her life to her wages,
finds both wanting and, bought out, stays put, scorn-
ful of herself for not deserving more.
The concierge at Le Régent is forty-six;
there fifteen years, widowed for one, behind

counters a dun perpetual presence, fixed
in sallow non-age till Marie talked to her.
I learn she is coeval with my friends.

3
I learn she is coeval with my friends:
the novelist of seventy who gives
us tea and cakes; the sister with whom she lives
a dialogue; the old Hungarian
countess' potter daughter, British, dyke,
bravely espoused in a medieval hill
town in Provence; Jane whom I probably will
never know and would probably never like;
Liliane the weaver; Liliane's daughter
the weaver; Liliane's housewifely other
daughter, mothering; the great-grandmother
who drove us through gnarled lanes at Avignon;
the virgin at the source with wedgies on;
Iva, who will want to know what I brought her.

4
Iva, who will want to know what I brought her
(from Selfridge's, a double-decker bus,
a taxi, Lego; a dark blue flowered dress
from Uniprix; a wickerwork doll's chair
from the Vence market; books; a wrapped-yarn deer;
a batik: girl guitarist who composes
sea creatures, one of three I chose,
two by the pupil, one by the woman who taught her),
might plunge her arms to the elbows, might shy stones,
might stay shy. I'll see her in ten days.
Sometimes she still swims at my center; sometimes
she is a four-year-old an ocean away

and I am on vertiginous terrain
where I am nobody's mother and nobody's daughter.

5
"Where I am, nobody's mother and nobody's daughter
can find me," words of a woman in pain
or self-blame, obsessed with an absent or present man,
blindfolded, crossing two swords, her back to the water.
The truth is, I wake up with lust and loss
and only half believe in something better;
the truth is that I still write twelve-page letters
and blame my acne and my flabby ass
that I am thirty-five and celibate.
Women are lustful and fickle and all alike,
say the hand-laid flower-pressed sheets at the papermill.
I pay attention to what lies they tell
us here, but at the flowered lip, hesitate,
one of the tamed girls stopped at the edge to look.

6
One of the tamed girls stopped at the edge to look
at her self in the water, genital self that stains
and stinks, that is synonymous with drains,
wounds, pettiness, stupidity, rebuke.
The pool creates itself, cleansed, puissant, deep
as magma, maker, genetrix. Marie
and I, each with a notebook on her knee,
begin to write, homage the source calls up
or force we find here. There is another source
consecrate in the pool we perch above:
our own intelligent accord that brings
us to the lucid power of the spring

to work at re-inventing work and love.
We may be learning how to tell the truth.

7

We may be learning how to tell the truth.
Distracted by a cinematic sky,
Paris below two dozen shades of grey,
in borrowed rooms we couldn't afford, we both
work over words till we can tell ourselves
what we saw. I get up at eight, go down
to buy fresh croissants, put a saucepan on
and brew first shared coffee. The water solves
itself, salves us. Sideways, hugging the bank,
two stocky women helped each other, drank
from leathery cupped palms. We make our own
descent downstream, getting our shoes wet, care-
fully hoist cold handsful from a crevice where
azure striation swirls beyond the stones.

WILLIAM MEREDITH

Parents 180

What it must be like to be an angel
or a squirrel, we can imagine sooner.

The last time we go to bed good,
they are there, lying about darkness.

They dandle us once too often,
these friends who become our enemies.

Suddenly one day, their juniors
are as old as we yearn to be.

They get wrinkles where it is better
smooth, odd coughs, and smells.

It is grotesque how they go on
loving us, we go on loving them.

The effrontery, barely imaginable,
of having caused us. And of how.

Their lives: surely
we can do better than that.

This goes on for a long time. Everything
they do is wrong, and the worst thing,

they all do it, is to die,
taking with them the last explanation,

how we came out of the wet sea
or wherever they got us from,

taking the last link
of that chain with them.

Father, mother, we cry, wrinkling,
to our uncomprehending children and grandchildren.

MARK STRAND

My Mother on an Evening in Late Summer 182

1
When the moon appears
and a few wind-stricken barns stand out
in the low-domed hills
and shine with a light
that is veiled and dust-filled
and that floats upon the fields,
my mother, with her hair in a bun,
her face in shadow, and the smoke
from her cigarette coiling close
to the faint yellow sheen of her dress,
stands near the house
and watches the seepage of late light
down through the sedges,
the last gray islands of cloud
taken from view, and the wind
ruffling the moon's ash-colored coat
on the black bay.

2
Soon the house, with its shades drawn closed, will send
small carpets of lampglow
into the haze and the bay
will begin its loud heaving
and the pines, frayed finials
climbing the hill, will seem to graze
the dim cinders of heaven.
And my mother will stare into the starlanes,
the endless tunnels of nothing,
and as she gazes,
under the hour's spell,
she will think how we yield each night
to the soundless storms of decay

that tear at the folding flesh,
and she will not know
why she is here
or what she is prisoner of
if not the conditions of love that brought her to this.

3
My mother will go indoors
and the fields, the bare stones
will drift in peace, small creatures—
the mouse and the swift—will sleep
at opposite ends of the house.
Only the cricket will be up,
repeating its one shrill note
to the rotten boards of the porch,
to the rusted screens, to the air, to the rimless dark,
to the sea that keeps to itself.
Why should my mother awake?
The earth is not yet a garden
about to be turned. The stars
are not yet bells that ring
at night for the lost.
It is much too late.

This year,
I'm raising the emotional ante,
putting my face
in the leaves to be stepped on,
seeing myself among them, that is;
that is, likening
leaf-vein to artery, leaf to flesh,
the passage of a leaf in autumn
to the passage of autumn,
branch-tip and winter spaces
to possibilities, and possibility
to God. Even on East 61st Street
in the blowzy city of New York,
someone has planted a gingko
because it has leaves like fans like hands,
hand-leaves, and sex. Those lovely
Chinese hands on the sidewalks
so far from delicacy
or even, perhaps, another gender of gingko—
do we see them?
No one ever treated us so gently
as these green-going-to-yellow hands
fanned out where we walk.
No one ever fell down so quietly
and lay where we would look
when we were tired or embarrassed,
or so bowed down by humanity
that we had to watch out lest our shoes stumble,
and looked down not to look up
until something looked like parts of people
where we were walking. We have no
experience to make us see the gingko
or any other tree,

and, in our admiration for whatever grows tall
and outlives us,
we look away, or look at the middles of things,
which would not be our way
if we truly thought we were gods.

III. Blue

Everyone is gone. Everyone.
At a gutted store building
in his old neighborhood
Willie idles, kicking the rubbish.
By chance the odd pieces gather
into a stick figure—a boy.
Willie adds bits of cloth
and an old mop head for hair,
but he finds no object to be
a word to coax his boy to talk.
The face is a cracked white plate.
Willie throws it in the road
hoping a tire explodes.
The image exists when it confirms
our sense of being. Willie feels blue
like the sky, so close so far away.
When he opens his mouth
there is no sound but a window
opened wide to show more air.

EDWARD HIRSCH

Tonight I want to say something wonderful
for the sleepwalkers who have so much faith
in their legs, so much faith in the invisible

arrow carved into the carpet, the worn path
that leads to the stairs instead of the window,
the gaping doorway instead of the seamless mirror.

I love the way that sleepwalkers are willing
to step out of their bodies into the night,
to raise their arms and welcome the darkness,

palming the blank spaces, touching everything.
Always they return home safely, like blind men
who know it is morning by feeling shadows.

And always they wake up as themselves again.
That's why I want to say something astonishing
like: *Our hearts are leaving our bodies.*

Our hearts are thirsty black handkerchiefs
flying through the trees at night, soaking up
the darkest beams of moonlight, the music

of owls, the motion of wind-torn branches.
And now our hearts are thick black fists
flying back to the glove of our chests.

We have to learn to trust our hearts like that.
We have to learn the desperate faith of sleep-
walkers who rise out of their calm beds

and walk through the skin of another life.
We have to drink the stupefying cup of darkness
and wake up to ourselves, nourished and surprised.

Yes, I only got here on my own.
Nothing miraculous. An old woman
opened her door expecting the milk,
and there I was, seven years old, with
a bulging suitcase of wet cardboard
and my hair plastered down and stiff
in the cold. She didn't say, "Come in,"
she didn't say anything. Her luck
had always been bad, so she stood
to one side and let me pass, trailing
the unmistakable aroma of badger
which she mistook for my underwear,
and so she looked upward, not
to heaven but to the cracked ceiling
her husband had promised to mend,
and she sighed for the first time
in my life that sigh which would tell
me what was for dinner. I found my room
and spread my things on the sagging bed:
the bright ties and candy-striped shirts,
the knife to cut bread, the stuffed weasel
to guard the window, the silver spoon
to turn my tea, the pack of cigarettes
for the life ahead, and at last
the little collection of worn-out books
from which I would choose my only name—
Morgan the Pirate, Jack Dempsey, the Prince
of Wales. I chose Abraham Plain
and went off to school wearing a cap
that said "Ford" in the right script.
The teachers were soft-spoken women
smelling like washed babies and the students
fierce as lost dogs, but they all hushed

in wonder when I named the 400 angels
of death, the planets sighted and unsighted,
the moment at which creation would turn
to burned feathers and blow every which way
in the winds of shock. I sat down
and the room grew quiet and warm. My eyes
asked me to close them. I did, and so
I discovered the beauty of sleep and that
to get ahead I need only say I was there,
and everything would open as the darkness
in my silent head opened onto seascapes
at the other end of the world, waves
breaking into mountains of froth, the sand
running back to become the salt savor
of the infinite. Mrs. Tarbox woke me
for lunch—a tiny container of milk
and chocolate cookies in the shape of Michigan.
Of course I went home at 3:30, with
the bells ringing behind me and four stars
in my notebook and drinking companions
on each arm. If you had been there
in your yellow harness and bright hat
directing traffic you would never
have noticed me—my clothes shabby
and my eyes bright—; to you I'd have been
just an ordinary kid. Sure, now you
know, now it's obvious, what with the light
of the Lord streaming through the nine
windows of my soul and the music of rain
following in my wake and the ordinary air
on fire every blessed day I waken the world.

No matter how hard I listen, the wind speaks
One syllable, which has no comfort in it—
Only a rasping of air through the dead elm.

Once a poet told me of his friend who was torn apart
By two pigs in a field in Poland. The man
Was a prisoner of the Nazis, and they watched,
He said, with interest and a drunken approval . . .
If terror is a state of complete understanding,

Then there was probably a point at which the man
Went mad, and felt nothing, though certainly
He understood everything that was there: after all,
He could see blood splash beneath him on the stubble,
He could hear singing float toward him from the barracks.

And though I don't know much about madness,
I know it lives in the thin body like a harp
Behind the rib cage. It makes it painful to move.
And when you kneel in madness your knees are glass,
And so you must stand up again with great care.

Maybe this wind was what he heard in 1941.
Maybe I have raised a dead man into this air,
And now I will have to bury him inside my body,
And breathe him in, and do nothing but listen—
Until I hear the black blood rushing over
The stone of my skull, and believe it is music.

But some things are not possible on the earth.
And that is why people make poems about the dead.
And the dead watch over them, until they are finished:
Until their hands feel like glass on the page,
And snow collects in the blind eyes of statues.

GERALD STERN

I Remember Galileo

I remember Galileo describing the mind
as a piece of paper blown around by the wind,
and I loved the sight of it sticking to a tree
or jumping into the back seat of a car,
and for years I watched paper leap through my cities;
but yesterday I saw the mind was a squirrel caught
    crossing
Route 80 between the wheels of a giant truck,
dancing back and forth like a thin leaf,
or a frightened string, for only two seconds living
on the white concrete before he got away,
his life shortened by all that terror, his head
jerking, his yellow teeth ground down to dust.

It was the speed of the squirrel and his lowness to the
    ground,
his great purpose and the alertness of his dancing,
that showed me the difference between him and paper.
Paper will do in theory, when there is time
to sit back in a metal chair and study shadows;
but for this life I need a squirrel,
his clawed feet spread, his whole soul quivering,
the hot wind rushing through his hair,
the loud noise shaking him from head to tail.
    O philosophical mind, O mind of paper, I need a
        squirrel
finishing his wild dash across the highway,
rushing up his green ungoverned hillside.

MICHAEL VAN WALLEGHEN

Driving into Enid

—for Louis Jenkins

Hundreds of migrating hawks are roosting in the hedgerows around Enid, Oklahoma. If the sun were out you could see they were a reddish-brown and had creamy, speckled bellies. But today it's raining in Enid and the rain is mixed with snow. The hawks are merely silhouetted today, far off.

On sunny days, driving into Enid might easily remind you of a scene in a grade school geography book: behind the hawk on the fencepost, a train goes speeding toward some grain elevators on the outskirts of the city . . . then the horizon, and an airplane flying low over a few tall buildings. But today the winter grasses tremble on the hillsides and the scarce trees tremble.

I was just thinking I had come a long way . . . I was just thinking that next year, for sure, I'd buy a new car. I must have been thinking something like that on the outskirts, passing the first small factories, the ragged fields strewn with junk. . . .

Then, at the first stop light, some kid waves at me from the back seat of a police car . . . inscrutable, fierce. He looks like a kid I knew in grade school. His mother wore a fur coat in the middle of summer and believed the Russians were shooting tornadoes at us.

What did he do? Where are they taking him? They found him in a culvert trying to gut a chicken with a piece of glass . . . they found him trying to build a fire out of cow-shit and wet sticks. They found him alright and now he's going back.

Later on, I'll find his sister quite by accident selling cameras in the discount store. She has a crooked, shy face and reddish-brown hair. She's married now and her chewed fingers are tatooed SUE on one hand DAVE on the other.

PETER DAVISON

The Money Cry

My daughter cries when we have to talk about money.
"I can't help it," she wails. "I don't want to cry,
I just cry." How can a father blame her?
I set her straight by setting her allowance
or trying to mold the world to snug her budget
or preaching homilies about expense
and self-sufficiency. Foresight. *Foresight.*
All the while, quietly, helplessly, she cries.

Dollars of course can give a girl her head
with beads and shawls, or buy her sweet shampoos
and the acrid clangor of recorded music.
But dollars too could set her hands to work,
scrubbing pots and pans, mucking out stables.
No wonder money makes her cry! I can't
help wincing when I sit to pay the bills
from Progressive Oil or Dr. Leon Leach,
recalling the time it cost to raise the money,
and shiver when paychecks hiss across my blotter:
What will smear off? What is the handling charge?

I'd warn you to be wary of anyone
whose eyes light up at each percentage point
as though life were an electronic game
with nothing to describe it but the score.
The hunt's the game, not the computation,
yet all the while the world presents its bills,
and we sit paying them on Friday night
while everybody else is at the movies.
Listen! Don't cry. You get it and you spend it.
Take it and pass it on. That stuff won't kill you.

CAROLYN FORCHÉ

The Visitor 197

In Spanish he whispers there is no time left.
It is the sound of scythes arcing in wheat,
the ache of some field song in Salvador.
The wind along the prison, cautious
as Francisco's hands on the inside, touching
the walls as he walks, it is his wife's breath
slipping into his cell each night while he
imagines his hand to be hers. It is a small country.

There is nothing one man will not do to another.

BRAD LEITHAUSER

Angel

There between the riverbank
and half-submerged tree trunk
it's a kind of alleyway
inviting loiterers—
    in this case, water striders.

Their legs, twice body-length, dent
the surface, but why they don't
sink is a transparent riddle:
the springs of their trampoline
    are nowhere to be seen.

Inches and yet far below, thin
as compass needles, almost, min-
nows flicker through the sun's
tattered netting, circling past
    each other as if lost.

Enter an angel, in
the form of a dragon-
fly, an apparition whose
coloring, were it not real,
    would scarcely be possible:

see him, like a sparkler,
tossing lights upon the water,
surplus greens, reds, milky
blues, and violets blended
    with ebony. Suspended

like a conductor's baton,
he hovers, then goes the one
way no minnow points: straight
up, into that vast solution
    of which he's a concentrate.

MARGARET GIBSON

October Elegy 200

Precisely down invisible threads these oak leaves
fall, leaf by leaf in low afternoon
light. They spindle and settle.
The woods open.

Birds no longer
slide by without my noticing loneliness in the bold
stare of the night sky—a sphere
tight as an onion.
At night I wake to a cry like the tearing of silk.
I listen and listen. There is only an owl.
Again, owl. A dog barks.
A clock persists,
its parody of singlemindedness
heroic.

Then mornings, they begin in mists that lift
towards noon, but first as if you've dreamed them in a deep
breath inward the trees come shyly forward
like ribs. Then the doves,
their breasts the color of hewn
cedar, call and vanish.
No one, you beautiful one just beyond grasp,
slide your fingers along my arms
as gently as you slide down
oak and beech and shagbark
loosening the leaves.

Who's attached to you, *no one* . . . who could be?
In ordinary commotions of grief and joy
you're elusive, a radiance
that flashes so strangely different each time

or so seldom
we say of you, *once in a lifetime*
remembering perhaps a phragmite on fire
in salt-marsh light where river crossed into the Sound
or the blow of light that glanced between mother
and father nakedly, once. Just once
laying the fire, remember how I whistled,
myself entirely and no one?

No one would say this:
you may as well laugh in delight,
cut loose. Interpret in a moment's
surrender your heart.

I watch the oak leaves fall.
Surely by the time I'm old I'll be ready . . .
surely by then I'll have gathered loose moments
and let them go, no longer dreaming on the stair
sun-hazy, surely not the old woman who thinks that by
    ninety
she'll wake once, if a split-second only,
and live.

No one, if I were able to forget you, or find you, I might
    learn
to enter the cup I am washing, door I am closing, word
I am opening with careful incision, lover or child
embracing—
                    and fall towards that moment fire cracks
from common stones, a sunrise in evening.

WILLIAM HARMON

A Dawn Horse

Again the time and blood consuming sun crosses its corner
With a web of new born light
And there the last stars literally starve.

Grey among a hundred or so other greys
The dawn horse stirs,

Wakes to the waking manifold of new circumstance
And—totally inhuman and remote
Among deep empty drums of sound unreeling hungrily
As though long drowned or long ago
Among unsteady equinoctial darknesses—
Stands.

On the welcoming west slope of the world's first mountain
Half dark in the tilted dominion of imperial light and common grasses
He is standing up
As dew will stand on the difficult pitched deck of grass
In the looking light,

An ordinary model of simplicity,
Spotted
(As when water spots a smooth leaf
With many magnifying lenses
That evaporate in place
Or else slip in the inflammatory turn and sloping),
Cold,
Solid enough for anybody.

Not one that waits at a fence for forked hay
Or feedbag of fodder hung on a headstall in a stable,
It is only he,
The ghostly dawn horse,

Not maiden white but stone colored,
Not a martingale gnawing nightmare
Or rainbow shouldered unicorn at allegorical attention
Or one of those things with wings

But a shaking shadow
Like the remote beating of the timed beast heart
Begotten and blessed by something blooded and blood
loving;

Lowering his head for a moment
He starts to step.

Doctor, you say there are no haloes
around the streetlights in Paris
and what I see is an aberration
caused by old age, an affliction.
I tell you it has taken me all my life
to arrive at the vision of gas lamps as angels,
to soften and blur and finally banish
the edges you regret I don't see,
to learn that the line I called the horizon
does not exist and sky and water,
so long apart, are the same state of being.
Fifty-four years before I could see
Rouen cathedral is built
of parallel shafts of sun,
and now you want to restore
my youthful errors: fixed
notions of top and bottom,
the illusion of three-dimensional space,
wisteria separate
from the bridge it covers.
What can I say to convince you
the Houses of Parliament dissolve
night after night to become
the fluid dream of the Thames?
I will not return to a universe
of objects that don't know each other,
as if islands were not the lost children
of one great continent. The world
is flux, and light becomes what it touches,
becomes water, lilies on water,
above and below water,
becomes lilac and mauve and yellow
and white and cerulean lamps,

small fists passing sunlight
so quickly to one another
that it would take long, streaming hair
inside my brush to catch it.
To paint the speed of light!
Our weighted shapes, these verticals,
burn to mix with air
and change our bones, skin, clothes
to gases. Doctor,
if only you could see
how heaven pulls earth into its arms
and how infinitely the heart expands
to claim this world, blue vapor without end.

JOHN FREDERICK NIMS

Tide Turning

Through salt marsh, grassy channel where the shark's
A rumor—lean, alongside—rides our boat;
Four of us off with picnic-things and wine.
Past tufty clutters of the mud called *pluff,*
Sun on the ocean tingles like a kiss.
About the fourth hour of the falling tide.

The six-hour-falling, six-hour-rising tide
Turns heron-haunts to alleys for the shark.
Tide-waters kiss and loosen; loosen, kiss.
Black-hooded terns blurt kazoo-talk—our boat
Now in midchannel and now rounding pluff.
Lolling, we eye the mud-tufts. Eye the wine.

The Atlantic, off there, dazzles. Who said wine-
Dark sea? Not this sea. Not at noon. The tide
Runs gold as chablis over sumps of pluff.
Too shallow here for lurkings of the shark,
His nose-cone, grin unsmiling. *Cr-ush!* the boat
Shocks, shudders—grounded. An abrupt tough kiss.

Our outboard's dug a mud-trough. Call that *kiss?*
Bronze knee bruised. A fair ankle gashed. With "wine-
Dark blood" a bard's on target here. The boat
Swivels, propeller in a pit, as tide
Withdraws in puddles round us—shows the shark-
Grey fin, grey flank, grey broadening humps of pluff.

Fingers that trailed in water, fume in pluff.
Wrist-deep, they learn how octopuses kiss.
Then—shark fins? No. Three dolphins there—*shhh!*—arc
Coquettish. As on TV. Cup of wine

To you, slaphappy sidekicks! with the tide's
Last hour a mudflat draining round the boat.

The hourglass turns. Look, tricklings toward the boat.
The first hour, poky, picks away at pluff.
The second, though, swirls currents. Then the tide's
Third, fourth—abundance! the great ocean's kiss.
The last two slacken. So? We're free, for wine
And gaudier mathematics. Toast the shark,

Good shark, a no-show. Glory floats our boat.
We, with the wine remaining—done with pluff—
Carouse on the affluent kisses of the tide.

LAUREN SHAKELY

Definition

After our damp skins slid apart
I nearly starved, pulling
on my mother's drained tit.
She used all her strength
to shove me out of her body,
the last link stretched, slashed,
tied in a knot I wear on the beach,
flaunting the twisted emblem
of first rejection, the eye of flesh
that saw love couldn't last.

There was a roof over our heads
and that was at least something.
Then came dances.
The energy for them came from
childhood, or before, from the time
when only warmth was important.
We had come to the New World
and become part of it.
If the roof would shelter us,
we would keep it in repair.
Roof then could be roof,
solid, visible, recognizable,
and we could be whatever it was
that we were at this moment.
Having lost our previous names
somewhere in the rocks as we ran,
we could not yet describe ourselves.
For two days the rain had been
steady, and we left the trail
because one of us remembered
this place. Once when I was young
I had yielded to the temptation
of getting drunk, and parts of it
felt like this, wet and hot,
timeless, in the care of someone
else. After the dances we sat
like cubs, and cried for that
which in another world might be
milk, but none came.
We had only ourselves, side by side
and we began a wrestling
that comes, like dances, out of
nowhere and leaves into the night

like sophisticated daughters
painted and in plumes, but young,
a night darker than its name.
We gave ourselves over to adoration
of the moon, but we did not call it
moon, the words that came out
were instead noises as we tried
to coax it close enough
to where we might jump,
overpower it, and bring it to our
mouths, which is, after all,
the final test of all things.
But we could not, it only circled us,
calmly, and we wanted it more.
We called it Carlos, but it did not
come, we called it friend, comrade,
but nothing. We used every word
until we fell, exhausted, and slept
with our eyes open, not trusting
each other, dark pushing us even
farther into childhood, into liquid,
making us crave eyelessness,
craving so hard we understand
prayer without knowing its name.
At some point we failed
ourselves, and eyelids fell.
We dreamt dreams of even farther
worlds, so different they cannot
be remembered, cannot be remembered
because they cannot be described
or even imagined. We woke
and did not remember, and the night
before became part of those farther

worlds, and we did not remember
speaking to the moon.
We got up from the centuries
and centuries, and called
each other by name.
Honey, the one that was me said,
drying her tears that were
really the rain from the night
before, which had taken her
without me knowing, *honey,*
again, but she did not understand.
She wanted only the sun
because she was cold, she pulled out
hair to offer it, from her head
and her arms. She understood me
only when I held her, made her
warm. She reached to her head
and offered now me more
of herself. I took it.
I put it to my mouth,
put it to a cupped tongue
and took it in. She moved
and I put my hands on her knees
which looked up at opposite ends
of the sky.

We've hung David's *La Vierge et Les Saintes*
Near the piano. The companionable blessed
Surround the Virgin, her eyes are tolerant,
Dull with fulfillment. She is perfectly dressed,
Silk sleeves, green velvet gown, and jeweled cap;
Waves cascade down her back. Her Book of Hours,
Unlatched and lying open on her lap
Reveals white, distant, miniature towers
Against a sky of pure, medieval blue,
Rude peasants worshipping, broad fields of wheat
Beneath the sun, moon, stars. A courtly zoo
Feeds in the letters, magnified, ornate,
The lion, monkey, fox, and snakes twining
Around the words amuse her. She chooses not
To read just now, but touches her wedding ring,
And round her waist a gold rope in a knot.
From where she sits, her eyes rest on the keys,
Watching my hands at practice. She enjoys
Bach in Heaven, his sacred Fantasies
For her alone spin like fabulous toys.
Lines shift and break, she finds it rich and right,
Such music out of black dots on the page,
Symbols, the world a symbol from her height,
Great voices rising like smoke from time's wreckage.
Bach, like an epoch, at his clavichord,
Paused listening, and shaking the great head
He watched his mind begin, pressing a chord.
Tonight he would compose. Upstairs in bed
Anna Magdalyn worried, one o'clock
And him so tired, straining the clouded eyes to
Blindness; blindly for hours the master shook
The notes like legible blood-drops onto
The page, Europe a small book in his palm,

Giants in history's pages: 'Study Bach,
There you'll find everything.' And he worked on,
His wife awoke the first on earth to hear
These silver lines beginning, plucked, revolved,
Unearthly trills spiraling up the stair,
The night dispelled, Leipzig itself dissolved,
And Paradise a figuring of air.

CHARLES SIMIC

Old Mountain Road 214
for Goody and Maida Smith

In the dusk of the evening
When the goats come,
The two pale ones nodding as they pass,
Unattended, taking their time
To graze by the curve,
Its sharpness indicated by a broken arrow,
In the last bit of daylight

I saw a blonde little girl step
Out of nowhere, and bow to them, stiffly,
As one does at the conclusion of a school play,
And disappear, pinafore and all,
In the bushes, so that I sat
On my porch, dumbfounded . . .

The goats' intermittent tinkle
Growing fainter and fainter,
And then hushing, as if on cue,
For the whippoorwill to take over
Briefly, in the giant maple.

Child! I thought of calling out,
Knowing myself a born doubter.

GEORGE STARBUCK

The Spell Against Spelling

(a poem to be inscribed in dark places and
never to be spoken aloud)

My favorite student lately is the one who wrote about
feeling clumbsy.
I mean if he wanted to say how it feels to be all thumbs
he
Certainly picked the write language to right in in the first
place
I mean better to clutter a word up like the old Hearst
place
Than to just walk off the job and not give a dam.

Another student gave me a diagragm.
"The Diagragm of the Plot in Henry the VIIIth."

Those, though, were instances of the sublime.
The wonder is in the wonders they can come up with
every time.

Why do they all say heighth, but never weighth?
If chrystal can look like English to them, how come
chryptic can't?
I guess cwm, chthonic, qanat, or quattrocento
Always gets looked up. But never momento.
Momento they know. Like wierd. Like differant.
It is a part of their deep deep-structure vocabulary:
Their stone axe, their dark bent-offering to the gods:
Their protoCro-Magnon pre-pre-sapient survival-against-
cultural-odds.

You won't get *me* deputized in some Spelling
Constabulary.

I'd sooner abandon the bag-toke-whiff system and go
decimal.
I'm on their side. I better be, after my brush with
"infinitessimal."

There it was, right where I put it, in my brand-new book.
And my friend Peter Davison read it, and he gave me
this look,
And he held the look for a little while and said,
"George . . ."

I needed my students at that moment. I, their Scourge.
I needed them. Needed their sympathy. Needed their
care.
"Their their," I needed to hear them say, "their their."

You see, there are *Spellers* in this world, I mean mean ones
too.
They shadow us around like a posse of Joe Btfsplks
Waiting for us to sit down at our study-desks and go
shrdlu
So they can pop in at the windows saying "tsk tsk."

I know they're there. I know where the beggars are,
With their flash cards looking like prescriptions for the
catarrh
And their mnemnmonics, blast 'em. They go too farrh.
I do not stoop to impugn, indict, or condemn;
But I know how to get back at the likes of thegm.

For a long time, I keep mumb.
I let 'em wait, while a preternatural calmn

Rises to me from the depths of my upwardly opened
palmb.
Then I raise my eyes like some wizened-and-wisened
gnolmbn,
Stranger to scissors, stranger to razor and coslmbn,
And I fix those birds with my gaze till my gaze strikes
hoslgmbn,
And I say one word, and the word that I say is
"Oslgmbnh."

"Om?" they inquire. "No, not exactly. *Oslgmbnh.*
Watch me carefully while I pronounce it because you've
got only two more guesses
And you only get one more hint: there's an odd number
of esses,
And you only get ten more seconds no nine more
seconds no eight
And a right answer doesn't count if it comes in late
And a wrong answer bumps you out of the losers'
bracket
And disqualifies you for the National Spellathon
Contestant jacket
And that's all the time extension you're going to gebt
So go pick up your consolation prizes from the
usherebt
And don't be surprised if it's the bowdlerized regularized
paperback abridgment of Pepys
Because around here, gentlemen, we play for kepys."

Then I drive off in my chauffeured Cadillac Fleetwood
Brougham
Like something out of the last days of Fellini's Rougham

And leave them smiting their brows and exclaiming to
each other "Ougham!
O-U-G-H-A-M Ougham!" and tearing their hair.

Intricate are the compoundments of despair.

Well, brevity must be the soul of something-or-other.

Not, certainly, of spelling, in the good old mother
Tongue of Shakespeare, Raleigh, Marvell, and Vaughan.
But something. One finds out as one goes aughan.

MONA VAN DUYN

Letters from a Father 219

I

Ulcerated tooth keeps me awake, there is
such pain, would have to go to the hospital to have
it pulled or would bleed to death from the blood
thinners,
but can't leave Mother, she falls and forgets her salve
and her tranquilizers, her ankles swell so and her bowels
are so bad, she almost had a stoppage and sometimes
what she passes is green as grass. There are big holes
in my thigh where my leg brace buckles the size of
dimes.
My head pounds from the high pressure. It is awful
not to be able to get out, and I fell in the bathroom
and the girl could hardly get me up at all.
Sure thought my back was broken, it will be next time.
Prostate is bad and heart has given out,
feel bloated after supper. Have made my peace
because am just plain done for and have no doubt
that the Lord will come any day with my release.
You say you enjoy your feeder, I don't see why
you want to spend good money on grain for birds
and you say you have a hundred sparrows, I'd buy
poison and get rid of their diseases and turds.

II

We enjoyed your visit, it was nice of you to bring
the feeder but a terrible waste of your money
for that big bag of feed since we won't be living
more than a few weeks longer. We can see
them good from where we sit, big ones and little ones
but you know when I farmed I used to like to hunt
and we had many a good meal from pigeons
and quail and pheasant but these birds won't

be good for nothing and are dirty to have so near
the house. Mother likes the redbirds though.
My bad knee is so sore and I can't hardly hear
and Mother says she is hoarse from yelling but I know
it's too late for a hearing aid. I belch up all the time
and have a sour mouth and of course with my heart
it's no use to go to a doctor. Mother is the same.
Has a scab she thinks is going to turn to a wart.

III
The birds are eating and fighting, Ha! Ha! All shapes
and colors and sizes coming out of our woods
but we don't know what they are. Your Mother hopes
you can send us a kind of book that tells about birds.
There is one the folks called snowbirds, they eat on the
  ground,
we had the girl sprinkle extra there, but say,
they eat something awful. I sent the girl to town
to buy some more feed, she had to go anyway.

IV
Almost called you on the telephone
but it costs so much to call thought better write.
Say, the funniest thing is happening, one
day we had so many birds and they fight
and get excited at their feed you know
and it's really something to watch and two or three
flew right at us and crashed into our window
and bang, poor little things knocked themselves silly.
They come to after while on the ground and flew away.
And they been doing that. We felt awful
and didn't know what to do but the other day
a lady from our Church drove out to call

and a little bird knocked itself out while she sat
and she brought it in her hands right into the house,
it looked like dead. It had a kind of hat
of feathers sticking up on its head, kind of rose
or pinky color, don't know what it was,
and I petted it and it come to life right there
in her hands and she took it out and it flew. She says
they think the window is the sky on a fair
day, she feeds birds too but hasn't got
so many. She says to hang strips of aluminum foil
in the window so we'll do that. She raved about
our birds. P.S. The book just come in the mail.

V

Say, that book is sure good, I study
in it every day and enjoy our birds.
Some of them I can't identify
for sure, I guess they're females, the Latin words
I just skip over. Bet you'd never guess
the sparrows I've got here, House Sparrows you wrote,
but I have Fox Sparrows, Song Sparrows, Vesper
    Sparrows,
Pine Woods and Tree and Chipping and White Throat
and White Crowned Sparrows. I have six Cardinals,
three pairs, they come at early morning and night,
the males at the feeder and on the ground the females.
Juncos, maybe 25, they fight
for the ground, that's what they used to call snowbirds. I
    miss
the Bluebirds since the weather warmed. Their breast
is the color of a good ripe muskmelon. Tufted Titmouse
is sort of blue with a little tiny crest.
And I have Flicker and Red-Bellied and Red-

Headed Woodpeckers, you would die laughing
to see Red-Bellied, he hangs on with his head
flat on the board, his tail braced up under,
wing out. And Dickcissel and Ruby Crowned Kinglet
and Nuthatch stands on his head and Veery on top
the color of a bird dog and Hermit Thrush with spot
on breast, Blue Jay so funny, he will hop
right on the backs of the other birds to get the grain.
We bought some sunflower seeds just for him.
And Purple Finch I bet you never seen,
color of a watermelon, sits on the rim
of the feeder with his streaky wife, and the squirrels,
you know, they are cute too, they sit tall
and eat with their little hands, they eat bucketfuls.
I pulled my own tooth, it didn't bleed at all.

VI

It's sure a surprise how well Mother is doing,
she forgets her laxative but bowels move fine.
Now that windows are open she says our birds sing
all day. The girl took a Book of Knowledge on loan
from the library and I am reading up
on the habits of birds, did you know some males have three
wives, some migrate some don't. I am going to keep
feeding all spring, maybe summer, you can see
they expect it. Will need thistle seed for Goldfinch and Pine
Siskin next winter. Some folks are going to come see us
from Church, some bird watchers, pretty soon.
They have birds in town but nothing to equal this.

So the world woos its children back for an evening kiss.

DAVID BOTTOMS

In a U-Haul North of Damascus 223

1
Lord, what are the sins
I have tried to leave behind me? The bad checks,
the workless days, the scotch bottles thrown across the
    fence
and into the woods, the cruelty of silence,
the cruelty of lies, the jealousy,
the indifference?

What are these on the scale of sin
or failure
that they should follow me through the streets of
    Columbus,
the moon-streaked fields between Benevolence
and Cuthbert where dwarfed cotton sparkles like pearls
on the shoulders of the road. What are these
that they should find me half-lost,
sick and sleepless
behind the wheel of this U-Haul truck parked in a field
    on Georgia 45
a few miles north of Damascus,
some makeshift rest stop for eighteen wheelers
where the long white arms of oaks slap across trailers
and headlights glare all night through a wall of pines?

2
What was I thinking, Lord?
That for once I'd be in the driver's seat, a firm grip on
    direction?

So the jon boat muscled up the ramp,
the Johnson outboard, the bent frame of the wrecked
    Harley

chained for so long to the back fence,
the scarred desk, the bookcases and books,
the mattress and box springs,
a broken turntable, a Pioneer amp, a pair
of three-way speakers, everything mine
I intended to keep. Everything else abandon.
But on the road from one state
to another, what is left behind nags back through the
    distance,
a last word rising to a scream, a salad bowl
shattering against a kitchen cabinet, china barbs
spiking my heel, blood trailed across the cream linoleum
like the bedsheet that morning long ago
just before I watched the future miscarried.

Jesus, could the irony be
that suffering forms a stronger bond than love?

3
Now the sun
streaks the windshield with yellow and orange, heavy
    beads
of light drawing highways in the dew-cover.
I roll down the window and breathe the pine-air,
the after-scent of rain, and the far-off smell
of asphalt and diesel fumes.

But mostly pine and rain
as though the world really could be clean again.

Somewhere behind me,
miles behind me on a two-lane that streaks across
west Georgia, light is falling

through the windows of my half-empty house.
Lord, why am I thinking about this? And why should I care
so long after everything has fallen
to pain that the woman sleeping there should be sleeping alone?
Could I be just another sinner who needs to be blinded
before he can see? Lord, is it possible to fall
toward grace? Could I be moved
to believe in new beginnings? Could I be moved?

HENRI COULETTE

Night Thoughts

in memory of David Kubal

Your kind of night, David, your kind of night.
The dog would eye you as you closed your book;
Such a long chapter, such a time it took.
The great leaps! The high cries! The leash like a line drive!
The two of you would rove the perfumed street,
Pillar to post, and terribly alive.

Your kind of night, nothing more, nothing less;
A single lighted window, the shade drawn,
Your shadow enormous on the silver lawn,
The busy mockingbird, his rapturous fit,
The cricket keeping time, the loneliness
Of the man in the moon—and the man under it.

The word *elsewhere* was always on your lips,
A password to some secret, inner place
Where Wisdome smiled in Beautie's looking-glass
And Pleasure was at home to dearest Honour.
(The dog-eared pages mourn your fingertips,
And vehicle whispers, *Yet once more,* to tenor.)

Now you are elsewhere, *elsewhere* comes to this,
The thoughtless body, like a windblown rose,
Is gathered up and ushered toward repose.
To have to know this is our true condition,
The Horn of Nothing, the classical abyss,
The only cry a cry of recognition.

The priest wore purple; now the night does, too.
A dog barks, and another, and another.

There are a hundred words for the word *brother*.
We use them when we love, when we are sick,
And in our dreams when we are somehow you.
What are we if not wholly catholic?

LOUIS COXE

Nightsong

Just as a year might end
the world tonight may die
around the darkside moon
with one wipe of the eye.
The world makes something to see
if we go out and look
at fields of snow and stars:
the ogle eye of Mars
throbbing toc and tic
burns red in the dark.
See how it all ends,
this time that was never ready,
this future that never worked
fallen into our hands
and our hands deadly
and the dead, friends.

J. V. CUNNINGHAM

To Whom It May Concern 229

After so many decades of . . . of what?
I have a permanent sabbatical.
I pass my time on actuarial time,
Listen to music, and, going to bed
Leave something in the bottom of the glass,
A little wastefulness to end the day.

Under clouds, at the tag end of August
all the splendid atoms
fly off into darkness. This

is the nick of time, our
fine tooth comb, it's nothing
doing, never too late—

And they kicked him out of the city
and kept him from voting
for saying the sun was no god
but was rather a hot rock
and larger, even
than the Peloponnese
(Anaxagoras)
which is no doubt what got them

—Paul Klee
his pale face like a peeled egg
behind that upstairs window in Switzerland
looking out on what?
looking down on what?
(gathering dust)

Stendhal
in exile, even at home
frenetically changing his name
the way other people change shirts

THESE PEOPLE
said Lord Byron, "these people
have an endemic incapacity

for telling the truth"
   (before they bled him to death)

and his name now, in Athens
has been given to a sidestreet
where they sell shoes (him being
a clubfoot—though that, in the long run
was thought less important
than his money)

O I don't want to paint great pictures
he said. In Greece
they don't understand great pictures.
I want to be famous, that's all
and to have all the newspapers talk
(he was 25)

And the phoenix flower died
(*phoenix* whatever)
that had lasted three months—

"Maybe someone they look at it"
Niko suggested. "One of the Spanish.
Or maybe George."
                                        And "You don't believe?"
when I looked somewhat quizzical. "In Greece
(triumphant)
                        is superstition."
—taxing my faith in the nation.

It's paint, said Picasso
counting his rubles.

—Stendhal with a face like a fried egg
Paul Klee changing names like hats
and Lord Byron, fleet as Nadia Comaneci

    —and the phoenix
    flower dies
    and will not rise.
    "Once you're dead."

said the grocer
not all the flowers or the greens
will make you up—
as they placed a wreath
on the grave of Venizelos.

In the night sky
the fixed stars
are like nails in the atmosphere.
They are not lanterns.

"The world is perishable"
said Anaximenes

"and shaped like the top of a table."

RIKA LESSER

Degli Sposi

Of us
not much is known.
Our lives were not
extraordinary.
Our silence seals
a deeper silence.

Sharing the single bed, how close
we lie; fingers curved over palms
whose fable reads: *conjugal bliss*
is possible.

How simple it was. It is.
But the secret's lost. That's why
you look to us, how we carry
ourselves, our smile. We live
in that space where all's yet
to become: embrace—a tenderness,
an expectation, myth, tentative
gesture preceding touch. Before
the shock of contact, when caution
counsels: Leave.

Not at all easy, this, to speak
of love. And to survive. Our skin
glows red with passion in reserve.
Unbridled, it would deaden every
nerve. Feeling—the reins, the check,
restraint, repose, out of whose thousand
fragments we are restored. Loving
each other even after death. As if
life were not, had not been, enough.

We touch, we hold, we keep
one another free.

ANTHONY PETROSKY

Jurgis Petraskas, the Workers' Angel, Organizes the First Miners' Strike in Exeter, Pennsylvania

Draped in khaki, Jurgis
who steals chickens
makes his way in the black dust
among the workers—so tired
and slow—trying to persuade them
that some abstraction is worth their jobs.
Jurgis with fireflies in his head.
　　The old women sipping from a little bottle
of whiskey shake their heads and pray
to Matka Boza, virgin of virgins,
to deliver us from this affliction,
this crazy man who tells everyone
God is not good enough to them.
The girls don't sing on the steps anymore,
Matka Boza, and all we hear is the tune
Jurgis's troublesome bones play.
　　When the sun reaches the highest place in the sky
everyone stops and eats while the good lord of the day
spreads his shadows over the dreams of his people—
the hot bodies in the mines, the streets
where nothing moves
until we stir like flies. Tomorrow
the angel of his own lord,
the weight of his passion, digs his own grave
inciting the miners to riot in Memorial Street
where the troopers kneel hunched over
their black Fords, tipped off, waiting.

Even the sky here in Connecticut has it,
That wry look of accomplished conspiracy,
The look of those who've gotten away

With a petty but regular white collar crime.
When I pick up my shirts at the laundry,
A black woman, putting down her *Daily News*,

Wonders why and how much longer our luck
Will hold. "Months now and no kiss of the witch."
The whole state overcast with such particulars.

For Emerson, a century ago and farther north,
Where the country has an ode's jagged edges,
It was "frolic architecture." Frozen blue-

Print of extravagance, shapes of a shared life
Left knee-deep in transcendental drifts:
The isolate forms of snow are its hardest fact.

Down here, the plain tercets of provision do,
Their picket snow-fence peeling, gritty,
Holding nothing back, nothing in, nothing at all.

Down here, we've come to prefer the raw material
Of everyday and this year have kept an eye
On it, shriveling but still recognizable—

A sight that disappoints even as it adds
A clearing second guess to winter. It's
As if, in the third year of a "relocation"

To a promising notch way out on the Sunbelt,
You've grown used to the prefab housing,
The quick turnover in neighbors, the constant

Smell of factory smoke—like Plato's cave,
You sometimes think—and the stumpy trees
That summer slighted and winter just ignores,

And all the snow that never falls is now
Back home and mixed up with other piercing
Memories of childhood days you were kept in

With a Negro schoolmate, of later storms
Through which you drove and drove for hours
Without ever seeing where you were going.

Or as if you've cheated on a cold sickly wife.
Not in some overheated turnpike motel room
With an old flame, herself the mother of two,

Who looks steamy in summer-weight slacks
And a parrot-green pullover. Not her.
Not anyone. But every day after lunch

You go off by yourself, deep in a brown study,
Not doing much of anything for an hour or two,
Just staring out the window, or at a patch

On the wall where a picture had hung for ages,
A woman with planets in her hair, the gravity
Of perfection in her features—oh! her hair

The lengthening shadow of the galaxy's sweep.
As a young man you used to stand outside
On warm nights and watch her through the trees.

You remember how she disappeared in winter,
Obscured by snow that fell blindly on the heart,
On the house, on a world of possibilities.

W. S. MERWIN

Yesterday 238

My friend says I was not a good son
you understand
I say yes I understand

he says I did not go
to see my parents very often you know
and I say yes I know

even when I was living in the same city he says
maybe I would go there once
a month or maybe even less
I say oh yes

he says the last time I went to see my father
I say the last time I saw my father

he says the last time I saw my father
he was asking me about my life
how I was making out and he
went into the next room
to get something to give me

oh I say
feeling again the cold
of my father's hand the last time
he says and my father turned
in the doorway and saw me
look at my wristwatch and he
said you know I would like you to stay
and talk with me

oh yes I say

but if you are busy he said
I don't want you to feel that you
have to
just because I'm here

I say nothing

he says my father
said maybe
you have important work you are doing
or maybe you should be seeing
somebody I don't want to keep you

I look out the window
my friend is older than I am
he says and I told my father it was so
and I got up and left him then
you know

though there was nowhere I had to go
and nothing I had to do

REG SANER

The Fifth Season

Up a ladder weightless as bird legs, thinner
than the indelible grass
where thistle leafs out, sizzling like bacon fat,
I'm re-ascending to heaven, getting back into management.

In no time I've persuaded underweight creeks to invest themselves
in the Green, the Yampa, the San Juan, the Gunnison
as they go bandsawing deeper into their canyons.

I feed a magpie on seeds wanting to fly.
I remind burrowing prairie dogs to exchange and dissolve
into offspring. I nudge cottonwood lint across the Divide
while its tree stays behind
riffling, lacing the San Luis Valley with plankton.
I stock the sky's night waters with dim barge-loads of turquoise
before lofting them southerly, just under the moon.

Off seasons? There are none.

I go round stuffing fresh meadows under old snow,
arrange high-country silences so comprehensive
that only in them can each smallest cony or pine finch
or pipit
take its place and be heard.

I make certain no note is lost. I traffic in light
the eye has not seen.

Out of stumps and trunks and fallen limbs moldered,
out of the white-bellied slugs, out of silver leaves

trilling sage stalks; out of bindweed
scribbling its inexhaustible phrases, the sulphur-flowers
yellowing wind, the daytime galaxies thicker than
    powder,
quicker than number; out of pollen scum
dusting pools in the rock,
I send a fifth season up in the sky, rising always.

Is my ladder still there? One rung at a time
I begin to step out of heaven, a cloud's possibilities
descending, as if some pure volunteer—or common
    starling
dead in mid-flight,
flashing dark color off preen oil
in wings barely stirring, whispering
ever so lightly as its slow turn falls
perfectly aimed
through air's open doors
toward the exuberant wreckage of August.

SHARON OLDS

First Love 242

for Averell

It was Sunday morning, I had the *New York*
Times spread out on my dormitory floor, its
black print coming off dark silver on the
heels of my palms, it was Spring and I had the
dormer window of my room open, to
let it in, I even had the radio
on, I was letting it all in, the
tiny silvery radio voices—I
even let myself feel that it was Easter, the
dark flower of his life opening
again, his life being given back
again, I was in love and I could take it, the ink
staining my hands, the news on the radio
coming in my ears, there had been a wreck
and they said your name, son of the well-known they
said your name. Then they said where they'd
taken the wounded and the dead, and I called the
hospital, I remember kneeling by the
phone on the third-floor landing of the dorm, the
dark steep stairs down
next to me, I spoke to a young
man a young doctor there in the
Emergency Room, my open ear
pressed to the dark receiver, my open
life pressed to the world, I said
Which one of them died, and he said your name,
he was standing there in the room with you
saying your name.
                    I remember I leaned my
forehead against the varnished bars of the
baluster rails and held on,
pulling at the rails as if I wanted to

pull them together, shut them like a dark
door, close myself like a door
as you had been shut, closed off, but I could not
do it, the pain kept coursing through me like
life, like the gift of life.

JAMES SCULLY

What is Poetry

We know it doesn't rhyme much anymore
but is it beautiful is it true
does it transcend the moment
which moment

or is it ironic, does it echo, echo what
does it have ears

at night whom does it adore
yet at dawn
what dream would it go to the wall for

or is it vituperative, why not
doesn't it express powerful feeling,
an overflow of feeling, is it sincere
is that enough

does it lay bare the soul
or explore the give-and-take of intense personal
    interrelationships
which persons, what kinds of interrelationships
work or play or
why one and not the others

is it witty, profound, wittily profound, profoundly witty,
is it avant-garde does it shock the bourgeoisie
who love it

or is it above the social arena does it circle the earth,
    a satellite with a proper sense of gravity high
    above the winds of fashion
who put it up there
does it transmit breathtaking pictures of a tiny earth

to a tiny earth
if not, is it a vision of eternity
tell us about it

does it make anything happen
or does it die to itself, till others notice the smell
is it shrill does its voice crack
or must it be a baritone of honey
does it give pleasure, does it teach, delight, uplift
whom does it persuade
whom doesn't it

is it a set of rules a code of forms
what is the principle behind the rules
was it handed down and by whom
or pieced together in a workshop too long ago to
remember
can it be rearranged on the shelf
who really cares
may it be dismantled

is it moving, either way moving
is it the imitation of an action
which action
is it a bunch of willy-nilly impressions
who is impressed

if it were a crib
would you trust your baby to sleep in it
bounce up and down in it
learn to stand up in it then
don't answer that

is it a world created by the poet
for the poet of the poet
does it exist for its own sake,
but if it's a way of breathing, whose way
do they smoke are they
breathing making love or getting off work

is it the ideology of a class or the puff of genius
genius for what what class
what are you talking about
is it a man speaking to men
a woman speaking to women
or universal human speaking
to no one in particular
that is, no one at all

is it a mirror held up to nature,
to human nature,
or is it an escape, is it
a mirror held up to nature, to escape human nature, or
a mirror held up to human nature
to escape human history

are you afraid of it
do you understand it

does it embody human values,
values as they are
or as they say they are,
which humans, which values
is it for or against
or does it take no position,

where did it go then
does it levitate, is it in heaven

is it then beyond all this
what is it, where, if you know tell us

but if you don't know
shut up, we'll understand

Transient Americans,
here we are once more,
coaxing our burden of possessions
into yet another house . . .
ruthlessly junking the excess.
But two treasures we'll never relinquish:

This bright blue ceramic thing
spotted with orange. It could be
a stubby snake with a thimble-bonnet
in place of a head. Or maybe the
carbon-smeared cavity makes it a
chubby tobacco pipe?

. . . and this mother-of-pearl lined
wooden leaf dish the size of my palm.

The sooty snake-pipe ringed with oozed
glue is our much-mended candle-snuffer.
Aran, age ten, made it for me.

After Thanksgiving dinner, when I blew out
the candles, my husband, Malcolm, scolded,
"Now look what you've done to this teak table."
Contrite, I said, "I need a candle-snuffer."
Aran touched the wax tears. "Mom, what's a
candle-snuffer?"
With an inverted spoon over the smoking
black wick, I demonstrated.

A week later, Aran entered the kitchen,
grinning, his whole face singing,
his extended arm singing,

and I took from his palm the Kleenex-
swaddled packet   and unveiled this
clay candle-snuffer   and the whole
kitchen was caroling.

In that moment, Aran was my father,
and it was my seventh birthday.
Grinning like Will Rogers, he was extending
a newspaper bundle toward me,
and wonky from measles, I saw in the core
three pink flowers such as I'd never seen
before   blossoms like baby cheeks
among quivering damp ferns. "Lady's-slippers,"
Daddy said, "from the marsh alongside the track."

"That's railroad property!" Mamma flailed.
"That's stealing!"
Pushing up his hat—just like Will Rogers—
Daddy handed me the bundle. "You hold them,
Mina, and I'll get the spade." And I watched
the bouquet, all but breathing.
"You can't transplant those," Mamma sputtered.
"They'll die. The sun."
Cradling the flowers, I followed my dad to the
north side of the house, where nothing grew.
"Get in here, Mina!" Mamma fussed. "The light.
I *told* you. Your eyes."
But I stood beside my dad while
he transplanted the flowers.

And every day I watered them.

"They won't come up next year," Mamma would
nag. "Don't be surprised if the neighbors
notify the police."

But they were up for my eighth birthday,
(I hadn't gone blind, and the cops never came.)
larger than before   plus a satiny white star
"A trillium," Daddy told me, and a small yellow
lady's-slipper, "or orchid," he said.
"Well, don't count on it next year," Mamma lashed.

She had flogged a piñata.

May after May
under papermill soot and Mamma's hectoring
and freight train smoke   the beauties sprang
up   bountifully   and always the bonus twins.
Seven   nine   eleven   lush pink pouches
and trilliums and yellow orchids.

Now for the leaf-shaped dish.

Scowling at a windowfull of these in an
imports shop newly opened in our suburb,
Malcolm scoffed, "Trash. I'd like to see
a stiff tariff slapped on those peon products."

A week later: December snowstorm, twilight
growing into dark. Tad's baked potato is
wrinkling in the warm oven. I'm wringing
my hands. Where IS that boy?

A stomping. A thumping. It's Tad,
his fair fleece snow-soaked, a soggy
brown sack in his blue clutch.
"Come here, Mom," he whispers, and I
follow his drowned shoes up the stairs.
His eyes gleaming like a saint's, his
stiff suffering hand extracts from the sack
"It's for Dad." the leaf dish. "Hand-made
in India. *Pearl!*"

I was in the presence of Galahad and
the holy grail.

I perch the leaf dish, as always,
on the top shelf of Malcolm's desk
in company with the Noh mask and African
ivory and Chinese Jade.
The candle-snuffer presides here,
between Malcolm's heirloom Haviland
and silver candlesticks.

I think of our lineage, usually,
as a skein of protein so widging and
widdershins that it's sagging towards
extinction.
I had forgotten these filaments that
flame forth, seasonally, to plait us into
the broad braid of humanity.

Only yesterday, Aran's girl-wife,
glancing toward the ceiling where the
bald light bulb had recently glared,

announced, shyly, to us, her brittle guests,
"Aran stayed up half the night making this—"
And the woven willow lampshade floated over
our Thanksgiving feast   like an angel.

We surmount our spoilers, sometimes.

Cold drool on his chin, warm drool in his lap, a sigh,
The bitterness of too many cigarettes
On his breath: portrait of the autist
Asleep in the arms of his armchair, age thirteen,
Dizzily starting to wake just as the sun
Is setting. The room is already dark while outside
Rosewater streams from a broken yolk of blood.

All he has to do to sleep is open
A book; but the wet dream is new, as if
The pressure of *De Bello Gallico*
And Willa Cather face down on his fly,
Spread wide, one clasping the other from behind,
Had added confusion to confusion, like looking
For your glasses with your glasses on,

A mystically clear, unknowing trance of being . . .
And then you feel them—like that, his first wet dream
Seated in a chair, though not his first.
Mr. Hobbs, the Latin master with
A Roman nose he's always blowing, who keeps
His gooey handkerchief tucked in his jacket sleeve,
Pulls his hanky out, and fades away.

French, English, math, history: masters one
By one arrive, start to do what they do
In life, some oddity, some thing they do,
Then vanish. The darkness of the room grows brighter
The darker it gets outside, because of the moonlight.
O adolescence! darkness of a hole
The silver moonlight fills to overflowing!

If only he could be von Schrader or
Deloges, a beautiful athlete or a complete
Shit. God, von Schrader lazily shagging flies,
The beautiful flat trajectory of his throw.
Instead of seeking power, being it!
Tomorrow Deloges will lead the school in prayer,
Not that the autist would want to take his place.

Naked boys are yelling and snapping wet towels
At each other in the locker room,
Like a big swordfighting scene from *The Three Musketeers*,
Parry and thrust, roars of laughter and rage,
Lush Turkish steam billowing from the showers.
The showers hiss, the air is silver fox.
Hot breath, flashes of swords, the ravishing fur!—

Swashbuckling boys brandishing their towels!
Depression, aggression, elation—and acne cream—
The eco-system of a boy his age.
He combs his wet hair straight, he hates his curls,
He checks his pimples. Only the biggest ones show,
Or rather the ointment on them caked like mud,
Supposedly skin-color, invisible; dabs

Of peanut butter that have dried to fossils,
That even a shower won't wash away, like flaws
Of character expressed by their concealment—
Secrets holding up signs—O adolescence!
O silence not really hidden by the words,
Which are not true, the words, the words, the words—
Unless you scrub, will not wash away.

But how sweetly they strive to outreach these
shortcomings,
These boys who call each other by their last names,
Copying older boys and masters—it's why
He isn't wearing his glasses, though he can't see.
That fiend Deloges notices but says nothing.
Butting rams, each looks at the other sincerely,
And doesn't look away, blue eyes that lie.

He follows his astigmatism toward
The schoolbuses lined up to take everyone home,
But which are empty still, which have that smiling,
Sweet-natured blur of the retarded, oafs
In clothes too small, too wrong, too red and white,
And *painfully* eager to please a sadist so cruel
He wouldn't even hurt a masochist.

The sadistic eye of the autist shapes the world
Into a sort of, call it innocence,
Ready to be wronged, ready to
Be tortured into power and beauty, into
Words his phonographic memory
Will store on silence like particles of oil
On water—the rainbow of polarity

Which made this poem. I put my glasses on,
And shut my eyes. O adolescence, sing!
All the bus windows are open because it's warm.
I blindly face a breeze almost too sweet
To bear. I hear a hazy drone and float—
A dimpled cloud—above the poor white and poorer
Black neighborhoods which surround the small airfield.

CHARLES WRIGHT

Two Stories

Tonight, on the deck, the lights
Semaphore up at me through the atmosphere,
Town lights, familiar lights
                                        pulsing and slacking off
The way they used to back on the ridge outside of
    Kingsport
35 years ago,
The moonlight sitting inside my head
Like knives,
                    the cold like a drug I knew I'd settle down
                    with.
I used to imagine them shore lights, as these are, then,
As something inside me listened with all its weight
For the sea-surge and the sea-change.

There's a soft spot in everything
Our fingers touch,
                              the one place where everything breaks
When we press it just right.
The past is like that with its arduous edges and blind
    sides,
The whorls of our fingerprints
                                        embedded along its walls
Like fossils the sea has left behind.

This is a story I swear is true.

I used to sleepwalk, But only
On camping trips,
                              or whenever I slept outside.
One August, when I was 11, on Mount LeConte in
    Tennessee,

Campfire over, and ghost story over,
Everyone still asleep, apparently I arose
From my sleeping bag,
        opened the tent flap, and started out on the trail
That led to the drop-off, where the mountainside
Went straight down for almost a thousand feet.
Half-moon and cloud cover, so some light
As I went on up the path through the rhododendron,
The small pebbles and split roots
                                like nothing under my
                                feet.
The cliff-side was half-a-mile from the campsite.
As I got closer,
                moving blindly, unerringly,
Deeper in sleep than the shrubs,
I stepped out, it appears,
Onto the smooth lip of the rock cape of the cliff,
When my left hand, and then my right hand,
Stopped me as they were stopped
By the breathing side of a bear which woke me
And there we were,
            the child and the black bear and the cliff-
    drop,
And this is the way it went—
            I stepped back, and I turned around,
And I walked down through the rhododendron
And never looked back,
                        truly awake in the throbbing
                        world,
And I ducked through the low flap
Of the tent, so quietly, and I went to sleep
And never told anyone

Till years later when I thought I knew what it meant,
which now I've forgot.

And this one is questionable,

Though sworn to me by an old friend
Who'd killed a six-foot diamondback about seven o'clock
in the morning
(He'd found it coiled in a sunny place),
And threw it into a croker sack with its head chopped
off, and threw the sack in the back of a jeep,
Then left for his day's work
On the farm.
That evening he started to show the snake
To someone, and put his hand in the sack to pull it out.
As he reached in, the snake's stump struck him.
His wrist was bruised for a week.

It's not age,
nor time with its gold eyelid and blink,
Nor dissolution in all its mimicry
That lifts us and sorts us out.
It's discontinuity
and all its spangled coming between
That sends us apart and keeps us there in a dread.
It's what's in the rearview mirror,
smaller and out of sight.

What do you do when the words don't come to you any
more,
And all the embolisms fade in the dirt?
And the ocean sings in its hammock,

ACKNOWLEDGMENTS

Special thanks are due to The Academy of American Poets' twelve current Chancellors, Robert Fitzgerald, Anthony Hecht, Daniel Hoffman, John Hollander, Stanley Kunitz, William Meredith, James Merrill, Howard Nemerov, May Swenson, David Wagoner, Robert Penn Warren, and Richard Wilbur, for suggesting the poems by deceased poets which appear on these pages; to Henri Cole, the Academy's Executive Director, for researching the lesser known poets, gathering texts, and advising in the final selection of poems; and to Paul Gottlieb, President of Harry N. Abrams, Inc., whose imagination and commitment brought this book to be.

The Academy would also like to thank Edith Pavese, an ideal and patient editor, and her assistant Margaret Rennolds, for their active cooperation and kindness in the preparation of this anthology. On the Academy's own staff, we gratefully acknowledge the work of Peter Batacan, Mary Busch, and Alexander Tulinsky in preparing the final manuscript.

CREDITS AND PERMISSIONS

Grateful acknowledgment is made for permission to reproduce the following poems:

"Grapes Making" from *Poems: A Selection* (Funk and Wagnalls Co.) by Léonie Adams, reprinted by permission of Léonie Adams. Copyright © 1954.

"Ice" from *Killing Floor* by Ai, reprinted by permission of Houghton Mifflin Company. Copyright © 1979 by Ai.

"Preludes for Memnon, II" from *Collected Poems,* Second Edition, by Conrad Aiken. Copyright © 1953, 1970 by Conrad Aiken; renewed 1981 by Mary Aiken. Reprinted by permission of Oxford University Press, Inc.

"For John Clare" from *The Double Dream of Spring* by John Ashbery, reprinted by permission of Ecco Press. Copyright ©1970 by John Ashbery.

"In Praise of Limestone" from *W.H. Auden: Collected Poems,* edited by Edward Mendelson. Reprinted by permission of Random House. Copyright © 1976 by W.H. Auden.

"Interval" from *Sunrise Trumpets* by Joseph Auslander. Copyright © 1924 by Harper & Row, Publishers, Inc.; renewed 1953 by Joseph Auslander. Reprinted by permission of Harper & Row Publishers, Inc.

"Flyfishermen in Wartime" from *Day of Fire* by Leonard Bacon. Copyright © 1943 by Oxford University Press, Inc.; Renewed 1971 by Martha Bacon Ballinger. Reprinted by permission of the publisher.

"The Guard at the Binh Thuy Bridge" from *After Our War* by John Balaban, reprinted by permission of University of Pittsburgh Press. Copyright © 1974 by John Balaban.

Marvin Bell, "These Green-Going-To-Yellow" from *These Green-Going-To-Yellow* copyright © 1981 by Marvin Bell. Reprinted with the permission of Atheneum Publishers, Inc. First appeared in *The New Yorker.*

"Jesse James" reprinted by permission of Dodd, Mead & Company, Inc. from *Golden Fleece* by William Rose Benét. Copyright 1933, 1935 by Dodd, Mead & Company. Copyright renewed.

"The Beautiful Ruined Orchard" from *Time Without Number* by Daniel Berrigan, S.J., reprinted by permission of the author. Copyright © 1957 by Daniel Berrigan.

"Dream Song #48" from *77 Dream Songs* by John Berryman, reprinted by permission of Farrar, Straus & Giroux, Inc. Copyright © 1964 by John Berryman.

"Poem" from *Geography III* by Elizabeth Bishop, reprinted by permission of Farrar, Straus & Giroux, Inc. Copyright © 1976 by Elizabeth Bishop.

"Evening in the Sanitarium" from *The Blue Estuaries: Poems 1923–1968* by Louise Bogan, reprinted by permission of Farrar, Straus & Giroux, Inc. Copyright © 1968 by Louise Bogan.

"Stove" from *Available Light* by Philip Booth. Copyright © 1976 by Philip Booth. Originally published in *The New Yorker*. Reprinted by permission of Viking Penguin Inc.

"In a U-Haul North of Damascus" from *In a U-Haul North of Damascus* by David Bottoms, reprinted by permission of William Morrow & Co., Inc. Copyright © 1983 by David Bottoms.

"Driftwood" from *Selected Poems* by Witter Bynner (Alfred A. Knopf), reprinted by permission of the Witter Bynner Foundation for Poetry. Copyright © 1963 by Witter Bynner.

"Transformation Scene" from *The Angled Road* by Constance Carrier (Swallow Press), reprinted by permission of Ohio University Press. Copyright © 1973 by Constance Carrier.

"At the Sign-Painter's" from *Work, for the Night Is Coming*; copyright © 1980 by Cheat Mountain Poets and reprinted by permission of Jared Carter.

"An Old Woman of the Roads" by Padraic Colum from *Wild Earth and Other Poems* (Henry Holt & Co., 1916), copyright by the Estate of Padraic Colum, reprinted by permission of Maire O'Sullivan.

"Rent" reprinted by permission of *Green House* and Anvil Press Poetry: London, from *Scaffolding: New and Selected Poems.* Copyright © 1984 by Jane Cooper.

"Night Thoughts" by Henri Coulette, from *The Iowa Review,* fall 1983, reprinted by permission of *The Iowa Review.* Copyright © 1983 by Henri Coulette.

"Nightsong" by Louis Coxe, from *The Yale Review,* summer, 1983, reprinted by permission of *The Yale Review,* copyright © Yale University.

"my father moved through dooms of love" Copyright 1940 by e.e. cummings; renewed 1968 by Marion Morehouse Cummings. Reprinted from *Complete Poems 1913–1962* by e.e. cummings by permission of Harcourt Brace Jovanovich, Inc.

"To Whom It May Concern" © J.V. Cunningham, 1983. From *Two Poems,* Chimera Broadsides, Series Two: Matrix Press, Palo Alto, California.

"The Money Cry" by Peter Davison, from *Poetry,* August 1982. Reprinted by permission of *Poetry.* Copyright © 1982 by Peter Davison.

"Earliness at the Cape" from *Collected Poems 1919–1962* by Babette Deutsch (Indiana University Press). Copyright © 1963 by Babette Deutsch. Reprinted by permission of Adam Yarmolinsky.

Stephen Dobyns, "The Delicate, Plummeting Bodies" from *Heat Death.* Copyright © 1980 by Stephen Dobyns. Reprinted with the permission of Atheneum Publishers. First appeared in *The New Yorker.*

"Animal" from *Poems of Five Decades,* copyright 1954 by Max

Gibson, reprinted by permission of Louisiana State University Press. Copyright © 1982 by Margaret Gibson.

"Beginning by Example" by Christopher Gilbert reprinted by permission of the author. Copyright © 1981 by Christopher Gilbert. First appeared in *Tendril*, Summer 1981, No. 11.

"The Two-Headed Calf" by Laura Gilpin, Copyright © 1976 by Transatlantic Review, from *The Hocus-Pocus of the Universe* by Laura Gilpin. Reprinted by permission of Doubleday & Company, Inc.

"Anachronism" reprinted from *Collected Poems* by Oliver St. John Gogarty by permission of Devin Adair copyright 1954, renewed 1982.

"Elegy and Flame" from *Another Look* by Horace Gregory. Copyright © 1973, 1974, 1975, 1976 by Horace Gregory. Reprinted by permission of Holt, Rinehart and Winston, Publishers.

"La Fontaine de Vaucluse" from *Taking Notice* by Marilyn Hacker. Reprinted by permission of Alfred A. Knopf. Copyright © 1980 by Marilyn Hacker.

"Ox Cart Man" from *Kicking the Leaves* by Donald Hall (Harper & Row, 1978), reprinted by permission of the author. Originally appeared in *The New Yorker*. © 1978 by Donald Hall.

"Lighting the Night Sky" reprinted from *Lighting the Night Sky* by Kenneth O. Hanson with the permission of Breitenbush Publications. Copyright © 1983 by Kenneth O. Hanson.

"A Dawn Horse" from *One Long Poem* by William Harmon, reprinted by permission of Louisiana State University Press. Copyright © 1982 by William Harmon.

"Locus" is reprinted from *Angel of Ascent, New and Selected Poems* by Robert Hayden, by permission of Liveright Publishing Corporation. Copyright © 1975, 1972, 1970, 1966 by Robert Hayden.

"The Transparent Man" by Anthony Hecht first appeared in *The New England Review,* Winter 1980. Reprinted by permission of the author.

"Nocturne" from *Collected Poems* by Robert Hillyer. Reprinted by permission of Alfred A. Knopf. Copyright © 1961 by Robert Hillyer.

"For the Sleepwalkers" from *For the Sleepwalkers* by Edward Hirsch. Reprinted by permission of Alfred A. Knopf. Copyright © 1961 by Robert Hillyer.

"The Center of Attention" from *The Center of Attention* by Daniel Hoffman, reprinted by permission of Random House. Copyright © 1974 by Daniel Hoffman.

"Violet" from *Spectral Emanations* by John Hollander. Copyright © 1978 by John Hollander. Reprinted with the permission of Atheneum Publishers, Inc.

"Plans for Altering the River" is reprinted from *Making Certain It Goes On, The Collected Poems of Richard Hugo,* with the permission of W.W. Norton & Co., Inc. Copyright © 1984 by the Estate of Richard Hugo.

"The Offering of the Heart" from *The Wind of Time* (Charles Scribner's Sons) by Rolfe Humphries. Copyright © 1949 by Rolfe Humphries. Reprinted by permission of the Trustees of Amherst College.

"90 North" from *The Complete Poems* by Randall Jarrell, reprinted by permission of Farrar, Straus & Giroux, Inc. Copyright © 1941 and renewed in 1968 by Mrs. Randall Jarrell.

"Hurt Hawks" from *The Selected Poetry of Robinson Jeffers.* Reprinted by permission of Random House. Copyright © 1965 by Robinson Jeffers.

"Bus Stop" Copyright © 1966 by Donald Justice, reprinted from *Night Light* by permission of Wesleyan University Press.

"In a Prominent Bar in Secaucus One Day" from *Nude Descending a Staircase* by X.J. Kennedy (Doubleday), reprinted by permission of the author and Curtis Brown Ltd. Copyright © 1961 by X.J. Kennedy.

"Saint Francis and the Sow" from *Mortal Acts, Mortal Words* by Galway Kinnell. Copyright © 1980 by Galway Kinnell. Reprinted by permission of Houghton Mifflin Company.

"The Testing Tree" from *The Poems of Stanley Kunitz 1928–1978*, reprinted by permission of Little, Brown and Company. Copyright 1978 by Stanley Kunitz. First appeared in *The New York Review of Books*.

"Report from a Planet" from *Poems from Three Decades* by Richmond Lattimore (Charles Scribner's Sons). Reprinted by permission of Alice Lattimore. Copyright © 1972 by Richmond Lattimore.

"Angel" from *Hundreds of Fireflies* by Brad Leithauser. Reprinted by permission of Alfred A. Knopf. Copyright © 1982 by Brad Leithauser.

"Degli Sposi" from *Etruscan Things* by Rika Lesser, reprinted by permission of George Braziller, Inc. Copyright © 1983 by Rika Lesser.

Philip Levine, "On My Own" from *One For the Rose*. Copyright © 1981 by Philip Levine. Reprinted with the permission of Atheneum Publishers, Inc.

"For Zbigniew Herbert, Summer, 1971, Los Angeles" from *The Dollmaker's Ghost* by Larry Levis, reprinted by permission of E.P. Dutton. Copyright © 1981 by Larry Levis.

"For the Union Dead" from *For the Union Dead* by Robert Lowell, reprinted by permission of Farrar, Straus & Giroux, Inc. Copyright © 1964 by Robert Lowell.

"After Tempest" by Percy MacKaye from *My Dear Lady Arise* published by MacMillan Company. Copyright 1940.

"You, Andrew Marvell" from *New and Collected Poems 1917–1976* by Archibald MacLeish. Copyright © 1976 by Archibald MacLeish. Reprinted by permission of Houghton Mifflin Company.

"The Third Wonder" from *New Poems: Eighty Songs at Eighty* by Edwin Markham, reprinted by permission of Doubleday & Company, Inc. Copyright © 1932 by Edwin Markham.

"The Hill" from *Spoon River Anthology* by Edgar Lee Masters (Macmillan), reprinted by permission of Ellen C. Masters. Copyright © 1962 by Edgar Lee Masters.

"A Winter Without Snow" from *Scenes from Another Life* by J.D. McClatchy, reprinted by permission of George Braziller, Inc. Copyright © 1981 by J.D. McClatchy.

"Parents" from *The Cheer* by William Meredith, reprinted by permission of Alfred A. Knopf. Copyright © 1980 by William Meredith. First appeared in *The New Yorker*.

James Merrill, "Lost in Translation" from *Divine Comedies*. Copyright © 1980 by James Merrill. Reprinted with the permission of Atheneum Publishers, Inc. First appeared in *The New Yorker*.

W.S. Merwin, "Yesterday" from *Opening the Hand*, Copyright © 1983 by W.S. Merwin. Reprinted with the permission of Atheneum Publishers, Inc.

"Couplets, XX" from *Couplets* by Robert Mezey (Westigan Press), reprinted by permission of the author. Copyright © 1977 by Robert Mezey.

"Family" from *To All Appearances* by Josephine Miles. Reprinted by permission of the University of Illinois Press. Copyright © 1974 by Josephine Miles. First appeared in *The New Yorker*.

"The Cameo" from *Collected Poems* by Edna St. Vincent Millay (Harper & Row), reprinted by permission of Norma Millay. Copyright © 1956 by Edna St. Vincent Millay.

"The Jerboa" from *Collected Poems* by Marianne Moore, reprinted by permission of Macmillan Publishing Co., Inc. Copyright 1935 by Marianne Moore, renewed 1963 by Marianne Moore and T.S. Eliot.

"Monet Refuses the Operation" by Lisel Mueller, from *The Paris Review,* summer, 1982, reprinted by permission of the author. Copyright © 1982 by Lisel Mueller.

"Now Blue October" by Robert Nathan, from *The Green Leaf* (Alfred A. Knopf), reprinted by permission of the author. Copyright © 1950 by Robert Nathan.

From *The Song of Jed Smith* by John G. Neihardt, copyright John G. Neihardt, published by the University of Nebraska Press.

"The Makers" from *Sentences* by Howard Nemerov (University of Chicago Press) reprinted by permission of the author. Copyright © 1980 by Howard Nemerov.

"Cigar Smoke, Sunday, After Dinner" from *Collected Poems* by Louise Townsend Nicholl, reprinted by permission of E.P. Dutton. Copyright © 1953 by Louise Townsend Nicholl.

"Tide Turning" from *The Kiss: A Jambalaya* by John Frederick Nims. Copyright © 1982 by John Frederick Nims. Reprinted by permission of Houghton Mifflin Company. First appeared in *The Atlantic Monthly*.

"The Kiss" from *The Night of the Hammer* © 1959, by Ned O'Gorman. Reprinted by permission of Harcourt Brace Jovanovich, Inc.

"First Love" by Sharon Olds, from *The American Poetry Review,* volume 12, number 3, reprinted by permission of the author. Copyright © 1983 by Sharon Olds.

"Jurgis Petraskas, the Workers' Angel, Organizes the First Miners' Strike in Exeter, Pennsylvania" from *Jurgis Petraskas* by Anthony

Petrosky, reprinted by permission of Louisiana State University Press. Copyright © 1983 by Anthony Petrosky.

"Last Words" from *The Collected Poems of Sylvia Plath,* edited by Ted Hughes. Copyright © 1961 by Ted Hughes. Reprinted by permission of Harper & Row, Publishers, Inc.

"Villanelle: The Psychological Hour" by Ezra Pound, from *Personae,* copyright © 1926 by Ezra Pound. Reprinted by permission of New Directions Publishing Corporation.

"Judith of Bethulia" from *Selected Poems, Third Edition, Revised and Enlarged,* by John Crowe Ransom. Reprinted by permission of Alfred A. Knopf. Copyright 1945 by John Crowe Ransom.

"Strength Through Joy" by Kenneth Rexroth, from *Collected Shorter Poems of Kenneth Rexroth,* copyright 1944 by New Directions. Reprinted by permission of New Directions Publishing Corporation.

"Singing Death" from *Some Lamb* by Stan Rice, reprinted by permission of The Figures. Copyright © 1975 by Stan Rice.

"Lost on a September Trail, 1967" from *Whispering to Fool the Wind* by Alberto Ríos. Reprinted by permission of Sheep Meadow Press. Copyright © 1982 by Alberto Ríos.

Edwin Arlington Robinson, "For a Dead Lady" from *The Town Down the River.* Copyright 1910 Charles Scribner's Sons. Copyright renewed 1938 Ruth Nivison. Reprinted with the permission of Charles Scribner's Sons.

"Effort at Speech Between Two People" from *Waterlily Fire* by Muriel Rukeyser (Macmillan) reprinted by permission of International Creative Management, Inc. Copyright © 1935 and 1962 by Muriel Rukeyser.

"The People, Yes," section 11, from *The People, Yes* by Carl Sandburg, copyright 1936 by Harcourt Brace Jovanovich, Inc.;

renewed 1964 by Carl Sandburg. Reprinted by permission of the publisher.

"The Fifth Season" from *Essay on Air* by Reg Saner, reprinted by permission of Ohio Review Books. Copyright 1984 by Reg Saner.

"The Living Room" from *Portraits and Elegies* by Gjertrud Schnackenberg. Copyright © 1982 by Gjertrud Schnackenberg. Reprinted by permission of David R. Godine, Publisher, Inc.

"Salute" from *Freely Espousing* by James Schuyler (Doubleday), reprinted by permission of the author. Copyright © 1969 by James Schuyler.

"What is Poetry" from *Apollo Helmet* by James Scully (Curbstone Press), reprinted by permission of the author. Copyright © 1983 by James Scully.

"A Dimpled Cloud" by Frederick Seidel, from *Raritan*, winter, 1983, reprinted by permission of the author. Copyright © 1983 by Frederick Seidel.

"Definition" by Lauren Shakely, from *Sulfur #5*, reprinted by permission of the author. Copyright © 1982 by Lauren Shakely.

"Old Mountain Road" from *Austerities* by Charles Simic, reprinted by permission of George Braziller, Inc. Copyright © 1982 by Charles Simic.

"Old Apple Trees" from *If Birds Build With Your Hair* by W.D. Snodgrass, reprinted by permission of Nadja Press. Copyright © 1979 by W.D. Snodgrass. First appeared in *The New Yorker.*

"Gifts" from *Outsiders* by Karen Snow, by permission of The Countryman Press Copyright © 1983 by Karen Snow.

"Swans" from *Slow Wall: Poems (Together With) Nor Without Music and Further Poems*, by Leonora Speyer. Reprinted by permission of Alfred A. Knopf. Copyright © 1939 by Leonora Speyer.

"Spell Against Spelling" from *The Argot Merchant Disaster* by George Starbuck, copyright © 1980 by George Starbuck. First appeared in *The Atlantic Monthly*. By permission of Little, Brown and Company in association with the Atlantic Monthly Press.

"I Remember Galileo" from *The Red Coal* by Gerald Stern, reprinted by permission of Houghton Mifflin Company. Copyright © 1981 by Gerald Stern.

"Ants and Others" from *Heroes, Advise Us* (Charles Scribner's Sons) reprinted by permission of Curtis Brown Ltd. Copyright © 1964 by Adrien Stoutenberg.

"My Mother on an Evening in Late Summer" from *Selected Poems* by Mark Strand. Copyright © 1980 by Mark Strand. Reprinted with the permission of Atheneum Publishers, Inc. First appeared in *The New Yorker*.

"Speaks the Whispering Grass" from *Album of Destiny* by Jesse Stuart (E.P. Dutton), reprinted by permission of The Jesse Stuart Foundation, Judy B. Daily, Chair, P.O. Box 391, Ashland, Kentucky 41114. Copyright © 1944.

"Some Small Shells from the Windward Islands" from *Half Sun Half Sleep* by May Swenson (Charles Scribner's Sons), reprinted by permission of the author. Copyright © 1966 by May Swenson. First appeared in *The New Yorker*.

"Aeneas at Washington" from *Selected Poems* by Allen Tate (Charles Scribner's Sons), reprinted by permission of Farrar, Straus & Giroux, Inc. Copyright © 1937, 1977 by Allen Tate.

"Adam's Dying" from *Poems* by Ridgely Torrence, by permission of Macmillan Publishing Co., Inc. Copyright © 1941, 1952, 1980 by Macmillan Publishing Co., Inc.

"Telephone Poles" from *Telephone Poles and Other Poems* by John Updike. Reprinted by permission of Alfred A. Knopf. Copyright © 1963 by John Updike.

"The Seven Sleepers" from *100 Poems* by Mark Van Doren, reprinted by permission of Hill & Wang, a division of Farrar, Straus & Giroux, Inc. Copyright © 1967 by Mark Van Doren.

Mona Van Duyn, "Letters from a Father" from *Letters from a Father.* Copyright © 1982 by Mona Van Duyn. Reprinted with the permission of Atheneum Publishers.

"Driving into Enid" from *More Trouble with the Obvious* by Michael Van Walleghen. Reprinted by permission of the University of Illinois Press. Copyright © 1981 by Michael Van Walleghen.

"The Shooting of John Dillinger Outside the Biograph Theater, July 22, 1934" from *Collected Poems 1956–1976* by David Wagoner, reprinted by permission of Indiana University Press. Copyright © 1976 by David Wagoner.

"American Portrait: Old Style" from *Now and Then: Poems 1976–1978* by Robert Penn Warren. Reprinted by permission of Random House. Copyright © 1978 by Robert Penn Warren.

"Hippopotamothalamium," by John Hall Wheelock from *The Gardener and Other Poems* copyright © 1961 by John Hall Wheelock. Reprinted with the permission of Charles Scribner's Sons.

"Advice to a Prophet" by Richard Wilbur. Copyright © 1959. Reprinted from his volume *Advice to a Prophet and Other Poems* by permission of Harcourt Brace Jovanovich, Inc.

"The Mental Hospital Garden" by William Carlos Williams, from *Pictures from Brueghel,* copyright 1954 by William Carlos Williams. Reprinted by permission of New Directions Publishing Corporation.

"Two Stories" reprinted from *The Other Side of the River* by Charles Wright, by permission of Random House. Copyright © 1984 by Charles Wright. First appeared in *The New Yorker.*

"The Minneapolis Poem" by James Wright. Copyright © 1966.

Index

Includes the Academy of American Poets Chancellors, Fellows, and Award Winners Since 1934

INDEX OF POETS, TITLES AND FIRST LINES

(Titles are in italics)